D0142847

TOWARDS
A DYNAMIC ECONOMICS

Books by R. F. Harrod

INTERNATIONAL ECONOMICS (2ND EDITION 1939)
TRADE CYCLE (1936)
A PAGE OF BRITISH FOLLY (1946)
ARE THESE HARDSHIPS NECESSARY? (1947)

TOWARDS
A DYNAMIC ECONOMICS

*Some Recent Developments
of Economic Theory
and their Application to Policy*

BY

R. F. HARROD

GREENWOOD PRESS, PUBLISHERS
WESTPORT, CONNECTICUT

Library of Congress Cataloging in Publication Data

Harrod, Roy Forbes, Sir, 1900–
   Towards a dynamic economics.

   "Lectures ... delivered in the University of London
in February 1947."
   Reprint of the 1948 ed. published by Macmillan,
London.
    1. Economics--Addresses, essays, lectures.
2. Economic policy--Addresses, essays, lectures.
I. Title.
HB171.H28 1980   330.1   79-20398
ISBN 0-313-22089-1

Reprinted by permission of The Macmillan Press.

Reprinted in 1980 by Greenwood Press, Inc.
51 Riverside Avenue, Westport, CT 06880

Printed in the United States of America

10 9 8 7 6 5 4 3 2 1

FOREWORD

THESE lectures were composed during the autumn of 1946 and delivered in the University of London in February 1947. When I received the invitation to give this course, it seemed to me that this would be a fitting occasion for me to resume the thread of my thinking, which had been broken in 1939, and compose a recapitulation covering certain broad aspects of the development of economic theory and its application to policy.

I was conscious, however, of a handicap. The war had meant for me a total interruption, lasting for more than six years, to my reading and study. In the main my official work had lain quite outside my normal field of interests, although it was my good fortune to have the opportunity of following the Anglo-American discussions on post-war reconstruction closely. I was aware that important books and articles had appeared abroad during this period, and that, in the brief time available and with the pressure of post-war academic duties allowing little leisure, I should not be able to make up leeway. I owe an apology to those writers overseas whose recent contributions to the subject may appear to have been neglected in these pages.

The idea which underlies these lectures is that sooner or later we shall be faced once more with the problem of stagnation, and that it is to this problem that economists should devote their main attention. Meanwhile the period of transition continues to stretch out before us. Indeed now at the outset of 1948 the path still to be traversed appears longer than it did in the autumn of 1946. None the less it is my opinion that the more complex the problems of the transition become, the greater clarity ought we to try to achieve about the character of that more normal regime that we hope we are approaching, albeit haltingly. If we are sorely perplexed about the problems arising from day to day, that may be in large part due to our not seeing the goal of our endeavours clearly. If that is so, then it is all the more incumbent upon us to give our minds to the kind of problems with which these lectures deal.

A more far-reaching doubt may occur to the reader. If it is true that there is a secular tendency towards a decline in the propensity to save, and if the stress of the war has given a severe shock to that propensity in Britain, then it is possible that we here can look forward to a considerable period in which the inter-war difficulties due to over-saving do not recur. In fact, it may be that just when we have at long last become converted to the need for a " full employment " policy, no such policy will in fact be required, and that in Britain it will be possible to run a successful economy of free enterprise without those controlling devices for maintaining employment to which so much thought has been given! This is, no doubt, an exaggeration, since the problems of periodic depression will surely be with us in any case.

But the United States is not likely to be exempt from the problem of chronic depression. What happens in that great civilization is not only of inherent interest on its own account, but is of direct interest to the rest of the world, since our prosperity is interlocked. I believe that the following analysis is of urgent and vital relevance to the immediate problems of the United States.

Save for the addition of a few paragraphs which

elaborate certain arguments, I am publishing the lectures as they were delivered. I must express my gratitude to Mr. T. Wilson, who has read through the proofs and made a number of valuable suggestions.

R. F. H.

January 31, 1948

CONTENTS

THE NEED FOR A DYNAMIC ECONOMICS

THE title of these lectures[1] leaves me much latitude, enabling me to dwell on the ideas concerning economic theory and economic policy that have recently been occupying my mind. This seems wise in a course of this kind in which you will wish me to avoid the trite, if possible, and do my best to give pointers towards the future development of our subject.

I propose to lead into the discussion by referring to a topic which I have treated on many previous occasions, but briefly and without elaboration, and, perhaps for that reason, without, it seems, influence or effect on the course of current writing. This topic is the proper definition of the terms static and dynamic when applied in economic science.

I am convinced that an adequate account of the contents of these two branches of the subject and the correct charting of a line of demarcation between them should have beneficial results on the progress of economics, and that the absence of recognition of such a line, even of an understanding of the necessity for it, has led to much confusion and fallacy in recent work, particularly in regard to the trade cycle.

Now it is true that the use of these terms has recently become more and more frequent. But we have

[1] Originally delivered under the title of " Some Recent Developments in Economic Theory and their Application to Policy ".

I

lacked a full methodological consideration of their proper application. Failing this, their use may tend to make confusion worse confounded. Unhappily usage is slowly becoming crystallized in advance of this necessary preliminary consideration, and I fear that it is developing in a form that serves no useful purpose. I find much that is unsatisfactory in the tendency to narrow the scope of statics, by imposing ever more numerous and rigorous restrictions on the alleged sphere and validity of that branch, with the consequent danger that what is true, valuable and of practical moment in the traditional static theory may escape attention and pass out of view. I find still more that is unsatisfactory in the use of the term dynamic. I do not refer only to the vulgar abuse of the word — for the merely descriptive, for the empirical, for the phenomena of the short period, and, finally, for anything that is outside the traditional corpus — but also to its use by our most distinguished authorities, such as Mr. Kalecki and the econometricians, and Mr. Hicks. If a certain usage seems to be growing and developing naturally and spontaneously, it is usually unwise to kick against the pricks. Words are in some respects our masters. There may be more semi-conscious wisdom in a spontaneous development than can be precipitated by the deliberate and studied classification of a methodologist. A word is indeed in all truth one of those " spontaneous social products " so much extolled by Professor von Hayek, and I feel that I may be falling into the vulgar fallacy of centralist planning in seeking to impose my will on the development of language. Am I not threatening a cardinal freedom, the freedom of speech itself? It is quite certain that economists above all will refuse to be " serfs ".

If one strives to determine usage somewhat against the

current trend, it is clearly incumbent upon one to show a very good reason why. It is incumbent upon me to show that fruitful results will flow from the dichotomy as I seek to define it. If we let the words take charge and a dichotomy hardens on different lines, that may actually prevent, or at least retard, a general recognition of the dichotomy which strikes me as the important one. I can plead on behalf of my own view, though this of course should by no means be a decisive consideration, that it would provide a definition in the economic field analogous to the division between Statics and Dynamics in physical science.

Statics there is concerned with a state of rest. Now the word Statics being already thoroughly established in economics, we may properly ask in what sense a " static " economy can be regarded as analogous to a state of rest in the physical world. We do not mean by it one in which no one does anything at all ! That is indeed perhaps the unkind suggestion of those who have affirmed that the truths of static economics will only apply when we are all dead. No ; in a static equilibrium certain values are deemed to remain stationary in the absence of fresh disturbing causes. These values are the quantities of the various factors of production applying themselves to various kinds of output, the quantities of the various kinds of output forthcoming per annum and the prices of the factors and of the various kinds of output. Thus a static equilibrium by no means implies a state of idleness, but one in which work is steadily going forward day by day and year by year, but without increase or diminution. " Rest " means that the level of these various quantities remains constant, and that the economy continues to churn over. In a certain sense, therefore, there is movement — thus the analogy is not quite perfect — and this fact

3

may be responsible for the confusions that have arisen. But it is surely perfectly clear if we read the classic treatises of mature vintage, of Marshall and his American and continental contemporaries, that it is to this active but unchanging process that the expression static economics should be applied. If this rough statement of the field of application of Statics is accepted, and I suggest that it must be, then Dynamics would be concerned with an economy in which the rates of output are changing ; we should have as the correspondent concept of velocity in Physics a steady rate of change (of increase or of decrease) in the rate of output per annum ; acceleration (or deceleration) would be a change in this rate of change.

In economic Statics we take certain fundamental conditions to be given and known, the size and ability of the population, the amount of land, tastes, etc., and these are deemed to determine the values of certain unknowns, the rates of output per annum of each of the various goods and services, the prices of the factors and of the goods and services. In Dynamics, on the other hand, the fundamental conditions will themselves be changing, and the unknowns in the equations to be solved will not be rates of output per annum but increases or decreases in the rates of output per annum.

Having given this rough indication of the lines on which a demarcation should be attempted, I will pause to develop the point that the scope of Statics has in my judgment been too much narrowed of late. I believe that this arises from a certain tendency to denigrate the work of the older economists. Static assumptions are often made so far-reaching in recent discussions that a law based upon them seems incapable of having any application to the world of reality. And so the moral is that all these laborious researches and findings of the older school have little practical application and in fact can be largely discarded. If we seek to formulate a precise notion of the scope of Dynamics, to take the place of the vague notion that it stands for everything that is new and thereby good, this may serve not only to show us the limitation of Dynamics — though of course my whole argument will be that attention to it is of great importance — but also somewhat to reinstate Statics.

I am sure that Statics will remain an important part of the whole. The general case for Free Trade in its widest aspect will continue to rest upon the static analysis. The principle that it is marginal and not average cost of production that should govern the use of productive resources also rests upon it. We shall have to be particularly vigilant in regard to the practical importance of that principle now that the sphere of nationalized production or planning is becoming enlarged, the more so since we do not seem to be quite as rich as we should wish to be, and can ill afford the losses that neglect of the marginal principle must entail. I may cite some words uttered by Lord Stamp in this place as long ago as 1923, on the contrast between the administration of business and public affairs : " . . . the third economic principle is the principle of the marginal return. The business, as every student of economics knows, pushes its expenditure along a particular line as far as it is profitable to do it. . . . But that is not the principle of government; it never can be." Perhaps our friends in the economic section of the Cabinet Secretariat would not acquiesce in this wide sweeping negative. But it will take many years, perhaps decades, of powerful advocacy, to secure such a far-reaching and fundamental change of principle as is involved by the use of the marginal criterion, in all the detailed procedures of publicly operated enterprise.

Static economics gives academic expression to what the ordinary person has in mind when he talks of " economizing ", that is, making one's resources go as far as possible. While not suggesting that the classic definition of economics supplied by Professor Robbins as " the science which studies human behaviour as a relationship between ends and scarce means which have alternative uses " has no relevance to matters studied in Dynamics, I think that the central core of doctrine and principle which is related to that definition will continue to be found in the sphere of Statics.

As instance of the eroding process, tending to narrow down static economics, taking the life out of it and departing widely from the intentions of its authors, may be cited the notion that it has to make such assumptions as perfect mobility, perfect knowledge, perfect foresight, etc. For the purpose of making an intensive study of some particular special problem within the field of Statics, it may from time to time be convenient to make all these assumptions in order to isolate the matter to be considered. But from the fact that these assumptions are often made, quite properly, in certain exercises in Statics it does not follow that they are implicit in the general body of static theory or in the practical recommendations that flow from it.

For instance, it is quite wrong to suppose that in general there is any assumption in statics of perfect mobility. On the contrary the whole doctrine of international trade, a very key section of static economics, rests upon the assumption of immobility. And, as has often been pointed out, the principles enunciated under the head " international trade " can be applied to the internal economy, in so far as an observed lack of mobility in that economy warrants such application. In elaborating a compre-

6

hensive theory under the general assumption of immobility Statics is by no means departing from its proper sphere.

Nor again does Statics imply any assumption of perfect competition, still less of perfect knowledge. The efforts that some of us made in the early 'thirties to evolve a body of theory as regards the behaviour of firms operating in sticky markets with differentiated products were quite clearly essays in economic statics.

I suggest again that it would be wrong to regard change as such as belonging to the dynamic field. Problems arising from a once-over change can, I believe, be satisfactorily handled by the apparatus of static theory. It is when we come to a steadily continuing change that we have to consider a different technique. When a once-over change, say of taste, occurs, the familiar static equations define the new position of static equilibrium. It is a commonplace that the whole system is interdependent and that a change of taste in regard to one article may in certain circumstances cause a disturbance affecting every value in the system, and Statics is designed to handle this. It has been argued that these equations do not suffice to define the paths by which the various magnitudes move to their new equilibrium positions, that Statics only deals with the position at each end of the movement and not the forces operating during the movement or consequently the precise lines of movement. There is some justice in this criticism; but I am inclined to think, although I do not wish to dogmatize, that this is making much ado about a somewhat trivial matter. Of course, if it can be shown that owing to forces set in motion during the movement the new position as defined by the static equations will never be reached, the matter becomes important. The questions, however, of the stability or

instability of an equilibrium and possible regions of indeterminacy are studied by the static techniques. I am
inclined to believe that when a dynamic economics has
been developed — and our present difficulty is that it
hardly exists — it will be found convenient to leave the
problems connected with the movements to new positions
of equilibrium after a once-over change to the field of
Statics. Dynamics will specifically be concerned with
the effects of continuing changes and with rates of change
in the values that have to be determined. Where ex-
ponents of Statics make an undue encroachment is when
they try to analyse the effects of continuing changes by
methods appropriate to once-over changes.

Since change and roundabout production involve
uncertainty — and a once-over change generates more
uncertainty than a continuing change — I conceive the
theory of profit to lie within the field of Statics. I do not
see anything specifically dynamic, for instance, in the
theory of profit elaborated by Professor F. H. Knight.

The introduction of the influence of expectation is
sometimes deemed to introduce a dynamic factor. I
cannot see that this has good grounds. Expectation is
always one of the determinants of a static equilibrium.
A once-over change in expectation is no different in
principle from a once-over change of taste. It is, however, possible that when we have a well-developed corpus
of dynamic principles the most important part of the
theory of expectations will be found to lie in the dynamic
field. The determinant in a dynamic system will not be
the existence of a certain expectation or a once-over
change in that expectation, but a rate of change of expectation. This of course may itself be determined by
a rate of change in some other fundamental condition.
The effects of a once-over change in expectation are likely

to continue to be handled by the technique of static economics.

Greatly as I admire Mr. Hicks's notable treatise on *Value and Capital*, of which a second edition has recently appeared, for its elegance and its logical precision, and fully recognizing the wide range and interest of the contributions it makes to theory, I have to record that Parts III and IV, which allegedly deal with dynamic economics, do not fall within my definition of Dynamics. Throughout Mr. Hicks appears to be analysing the effects of a once-over change in fundamental conditions. There is no recognition that a different technique may be required for analysing the effects of continuing changes. And, while by his fine handling of the working of expectation elasticities and to some extent of lags (of which more hereafter), he demonstrates the possibility of adjustments not considered in traditional statics and warns us of the likelihood of instability in certain circumstances, his final goal is always to show what manner, if any, of stable equilibrium of the old-fashioned type will be established. There is no hint whatever that what we ought to be looking for, beyond or beneath the oscillations, as the proper or normal effect of continuing changes, is a steady rate of change in each of the dependent variables. It may be that in fact in an advancing (or declining) economy there is a persistent failure to achieve those steady trends of increase which the changing fundamental conditions require, just as in a generally static economy there may, owing to the continued impact of detailed changes or some oscillation, be persistent failure to achieve the stable equilibrium which fundamental conditions indicate. But just as it is important to know what the stable equilibrium would be, even if it is not achieved from moment to moment, so in the dynamic field it is necessary to know what the steady lines of advance would be, as a basis for analysing why actual lines of advance depart from them and behave as they do. Of all this there is no hint in Mr. Hicks's treatise.

I stress that his treatment of expectation changes both as causes and effects, which is notable and plays an important part in his whole argument, is definitely static in character.

He defines dynamic economics as that branch of theory in which every quantity must be dated, recognizing fairly that the dichotomy so generated has little in common with that of mechanics. The definition is an interesting one and I have the impression that it may well be a genuine mark of the study of oscillation. In Dynamics as I conceive it dating is no more necessary than in Statics.

In the formulation and handling of its subject-matter Keynes's *General Theory* is essentially static. Involuntary unemployment is indeed a concept alien to the classical system of thought, but it is a static concept. So is liquidity preference. Liquidity preference is governed by a number of fundamental conditions all of which may be deemed quite conformably with the Keynesian system of ideas to be unchanging, and the resultant effect on activity and employment may take the form of a stable equilibrium. Keynes has much to say of changes in expectation which lead to changes in liquidity preference, but on the whole his handling of these is such as to imply that they are once-over changes and his method of treating the effects of these changes is correspondingly statical. There is one concept, however, which plays a central rôle in the *General Theory* which is not static, and that is why the *General Theory* will not be fully satisfactory until it is brought into relation with Dynamics. While many of the restrictions which writers have tried recently to impose on static theory strike me as vexatious and wrong-headed, there is a more radical restriction which must be imposed but which is in fact less commonly imposed. Positive saving, which plays such a great rôle in the *General Theory*, is essentially a dynamic concept. This is fundamental. The steady continuing allocation year by year of one-tenth of income to house rent is not a dynamic phenomenon; it is consistent with the unaltered maintenance of a stable equilibrium of prices and rates of output per annum throughout the economy. But a steady allocation of one-tenth of income to saving is essentially dynamic, since it involves a continuing growth in one of the fundamental determinants of the system, namely the quantity of capital available. This must entail, even if none of the other determinants are subject to change, continued changes in the values of many of the dependent variables. In the dynamic equations it will be these changes themselves, not the values that change, that must be the dependent variables. In static economics we must assume that saving is zero. This is not formally inconsistent, although it may well be inconsistent in any likely circumstances, with a positive rate of interest.

It is not to derogate at all from the great importance of the advance made by the *General Theory* to say that it is imperfect by reason of the inclusion of this dynamic concept, viz., positive saving, in a treatment which in broad lines follows the method of static equilibrium analysis. The schedule of the marginal efficiency of capital seems in that work almost to be taken as a datum externally given and not dependent on the rest of the system, albeit subject to numerous changes from time to time; but these are all of a once-over character, and not continuing changes generated by the special nature of a growing economy. To put this in another way: Keynes neglects what is usually called — unhappily from the point of view of my terminology — the acceleration principle. I shall have to return to this matter.

I should like to point out in passing, lest I seem to be condemning all reputable economic work as undynamic, that the so-called acceleration principle is essentially a dynamic principle, since it regards the volume of demand for a new capital as a function of the rate of increase of the economy.

Trade-cycle theory is on the border line. Fluctuation does not seem in itself to be inconsistent with a long run constancy in the fundamental determinants. For example, harvest variations are always liable to happen. If these occurred within a frame-work in which the fundamental determinants, size of population, amount of capital, etc., were stationary, they might conceivably cause a regular periodic fluctuation in all the magnitudes of the static equations. We might also have weather variations affecting health or psychology, which might set up vicious spiral movements. In fine, a static economy may be subject to a trade cycle. But there is little doubt that the trade cycle we know is conditioned by its occurrence in a dynamic (growing) economy. In my judgment much of the trade cycle theory of the inter-war period, especially in the monetary field, fell into confusion for lack of a clear understanding whether its assumptions were static or dynamic or which assumptions belonged to which category, and arguments were apt to be vitiated by the intrusion of an extra dimension or its omission.

Recently we have had very important work by Drs. Tinbergen, Kalecki and others on the influence of time lags. The results achieved have been most promising. This department of study is bidding fair to acquire a prescriptive claim to the title of dynamic. As I have suggested, it is vain to quarrel about words. I do not myself think that it is natural to regard lags as in essence dynamic phenomena. I think one might well find that we had one set of lags and one kind of cycle in a stationary economy and a different set of lags and a different kind of cycle in an expanding one, and that lag study will fall partly into each division.

This brings me to two further divisions within economic theory which are different from but have relation with the division into static and dynamic.

There is the distinction between the study of partial equilibrium and that of total equilibrium. There has always, of course, been a theory of both from Adam Smith to Walras. Keynes is felt to break new ground with his *General Theory of Equilibrium.* He certainly broke new ground, but not in having a theory of general equilibrium. In this regard, however, there is a marked difference between his theory and that which grew up in the classical tradition. Whereas in that tradition activity as a whole was conceived as the result of compounding the forces at work in the establishment of all the particular equilibria, the desire for goods, disutility of effort, etc., in the Keynesian system there is a contrariety. In the classical system individual motives tending in a certain direction may be added together to make up an aggregated motive on the part of the economy as a whole. The most notorious case in which Keynes breaks away from this tradition is in that of saving. In the classical theory the increased propensity to save by an individual increases the aggregate propensity to save and the aggregate saving of the community. In the Keynesian system the increased propensity to save by an individual leads to less saving altogether. There is nothing at all like this in the classical system. This contribution by Keynes may well prove enduring.

There is nothing specifically dynamic in this idea itself. But it is likely to play a prominent part in the dynamics of a steadily advancing economy, when the theory of that comes to be evolved.

The other division to which I wish to refer is between those principles that do and those that do not lend themselves to econometric verification. Static theory lends itself rather poorly. It is not true to say that it does not lend itself at all, for we have Schultz's attempts on statistical and, I should add, static demand curves. A large part of static theory is of course merely truistic; it can be used to verify figures and cannot be verified by them. Similarly with Keynes's *General Theory* : it contains much that is truistic, and an alleged statistical refutation of some of the principles there set out would merely refute the figures on which the argument was based. Some of his global concepts do, it is true, seem to lend themselves well to econometric methods. There may be danger, however, in attempting to measure marginal propensities (essential static concepts) by time series derived from observations in an expanding economy. Kaldor, and, across the water, Hagen, both know quite well that they are on perilous ground.

I am convinced that economic theory will only make good progress to the extent that it can transform itself into econometrics. But econometrics must have proper tools. The Keynesian concepts are not enough. And the crying need is for the formulation of dynamic concepts and the enunciation of a minimum set of truistic dynamic principles.

I have proceeded far enough in a critical vein and must begin to make some constructive suggestions. What I hope to offer in all humility is only a beginning, a pointer in a certain direction.

In order to go forward I wish first to make a retrospect.

I should claim that the old classical economics contains in roughly equal proportions what I define as static and dynamic elements. The dynamic elements have dropped out of what we now regard as the corpus of economic principles. As the static analysis came to be refined and perfected by the use of the marginal concept and by mathematical expression, the dynamic analysis fell out of view. This may have been particularly due to the fact that Dynamics did not give such scope to the marginal analysis. The lapse of Dynamics from favour is most remarkably illustrated by Marshall. We know well how lovingly he treasured all the bits and pieces of traditional theory. He could not bear to abandon the view that the rent of land does not enter into the cost of production. Even the iron law of wages reappears ; its guise is softened and rendered kindly, but it is there all the same. To make sure of my ground I re-read the *Principles* before composing these lectures, and I can find scarcely any trace of that dynamic theory which occupied at least half of the attention of the old classical school.[1]

We may take as an illustration Ricardo himself. In his preface we can find the famous words " to determine the laws that regulate this distribution is the principal problem in Political Economy ". A modern reader is grammatically entitled to take these words as referring to what we now know as the static theory of distribution. But we should regard them in the light of the earlier words : " In different stages of society the proportion of the whole produce of the earth which will be allotted to these classes under the name of rent, profit and wages — will be essentially different ". If one turns back to the preface

[1] Perhaps I do less than justice to Marshall ; Dynamics might have appeared, after all, in the fourth volume which he never completed.

after reading the book one is certainly driven to interpret the first quoted passage in the light of the other one, that is, to interpret distribution in a dynamic sense, the economist's first task being not to determine how the product will be apportioned among the factors at one time but how progress successively reapportions the product among the factors. May I remind you of the bare bones of Ricardo's Dynamic Theory? It was a large part of his whole theory. The prime motive force for him was the tendency to accumulate. This may be identified with what we regard as saving, and is rightly treated by Ricardo as a dynamic concept. He is not guilty of the error which has crept into text-books up to the present day of bringing saving into a static system of equations. So long as there is any positive saving the shape of society is progressively altering. This tendency to accumulate has the effect, in accordance with the Wages Fund theory, which Ricardo held in substance, although not in name, of raising the market rate of wages. This, in accordance with Malthusian doctrine, would make the population increase. By the law of diminishing returns, the marginal product of capital and labour would fall through time ; but since the population increase would be geared to maintain wages steady at the subsistence — or, as in fairness to Ricardo we may call it, at the equilibrium — level, the share of labour in the marginal product would rise, the amount of real wages remaining constant. Consequently the real profit per unit of capital would fall. This is true whether with Ricardo we use a labour measure of value or an output measure. Rents meanwhile would rise. This is a complete, if crude, dynamic theory. So long as any savings exist the distribution of wealth continues to change according to certain principles — rents rise, profits fall.

The question was raised — what would happen when profit fell to zero? Long before this, Ricardo replied, the motive for accumulation would have been removed. Thus he contemplated the advent of a stationary state with the rate of interest still positive.

I need hardly stress how important this dynamic theory was in the corpus of doctrine then known as Political Economy. The practical maxim of Free Trade was derivable from static theory. Hardly less important in the minds of contemporaries were those two other practical maxims, (1) that saving by those of means would confer more lasting benefit on the labouring poor than charity, and (2) that the main method open to the poor for self-improvement was to raise their concept of a proper standard of living and by consequence reduce the birth-rate. This of course went with the negative doctrine that it is useless to struggle for higher wages by bargaining or legislation; one could only affect real wages by restricting the supply of labour, which meant holding the population increase in check.

It is difficult to assess the importance in subsequent history of these two practical maxims derived from the old dynamic theory. Historians following Weber have found more ancient and deep-seated causes in Puritanism for the high esteem in which saving was held during the heyday of capitalism. But surely a little may be allowed for the fact that well-educated persons in the nineteenth century cognizant with political economy found there the strongest possible endorsement for the view that saving was a virtue. Saving according to this doctrine was not merely a self-regarding virtue, but a humane virtue, tending more than any other form of activity to the betterment of mankind. As regards the second maxim, history has certainly taken the course prescribed by the economists.

The labouring poor did in due course begin to restrict their numbers; they could hardly have made the great advances recorded in the last half-century, had they not done so. Whether there is any link between the persistent teaching of the economists over several decades and the growth of the birth-control movement is more difficult to determine.

These practical doctrines subsequently passed into disfavour, along with the dynamic theory on which they were based. The dynamic theory was crude, in part untenable as universal law, and in part untenable altogether. But nothing has been put in the place of this theory (or of the maxims), and the corpus of theoretical economics that we teach to-day right up to and including Keynesian doctrine remains almost exclusively static. The idea that Keynes is more dynamic than Ricardo is the exact opposite of the truth.

This old dynamic theory had two aspects. There was (1) the theory of motive power, and (2) the theory of progressive redistribution.

Now it might be objected that there is no need to lay much stress on the second problem on the ground that this merely involves an extrapolation of childlike simplicity of the principles of static distribution. So indeed it appeared to in Book IV of J. S. Mill, who endeavoured, partly in deference to Positivism, to stake out the claim of Dynamics for separate treatment, and whose definition of it agrees precisely with mine. The lack of imagination shown in his treatment, and his almost exclusive attention to the Malthusian principle, may have been responsible for his failure to secure a permanent place for Dynamics in our corpus of doctrine. I submit that there is more in this problem than Mill showed. In static theory we emphasize the interdependence of the whole pricing process and the requirement that the equilibrium should be stable. In a dynamic system the quantity of resources devoted to production is steadily growing (or shrinking) and we must examine critically the mutual dependence of the steadily changing volumes of supply of each factor and the steadily changing rates of remuneration. We cannot just assume that the introduction of movement does not introduce a new set of problems.

In the old economics accumulation was the motive power. Here we have a stark contradiction to Keynesian doctrine in which saving is always tending to retard advance. This problem will have to be reconsidered from the beginning.

Confronted with the mental habit, engendered by neglect of the subject over a number of decades, of supposing that there is no problem here of great interest or difficulty, I urge my opinion that this ground is very slippery and treacherous, and that most careful study of apparently simple matters is necessary. As a beginning, therefore, I want to examine certain matters which are more simple than either of the two problems I have just referred to, namely the necessary relations between the rates of growth of the different elements in a growing economy.

In this approach there are two propositions in the classical system which can be tentatively discarded. One is the population doctrine, the proposition that the supply of labour is infinitely elastic at a certain real wage, that wage being determined by what the labouring classes of the country regard as their minimum standard of living with sufficient firmness to influence their conduct in reproduction. This doctrine may still have relevance to large poverty-stricken areas of the world of to-day. It is one of the doctrines that may perhaps be regarded as valid in relation to certain circumstances although not universally valid. I am interested now particularly in the economies of the United States, Great Britain, Western Europe and other advanced countries. In this context we may regard the size of the population not, as in the old classical system, as a dependent but as an independent variable. To put the matter otherwise, changes in it may be regarded as exogenous changes.

Secondly, I propose to discard the law of diminishing returns from the land as a primary determinant in a progressive economy. Not that there was any fallacy in the classical treatment of this subject. I discard it only because in our particular context it appears that its influence may be quantitatively unimportant. I shall endeavour to define my terms, however, so as to leave room for any influence that it may have.

In examining an expanding economy we may consider the inter-relations between the expansion in three fundamental elements, viz. (1) man-power, (2) output or income per head and (3) quantity of capital available.

One might define a static economy by saying that these three quantities are assumed to be constant. The three being constant, saving per annum would be zero. Such a definition is perhaps unnecessarily rigid. It is desirable to make the definition of a stationary state as flexible as possible. The definition given may be modified in the direction not only of greater flexibility but also of greater precision by taking not the supplies but the supply schedules of man-power and capital as constant. On the assumption thus modified an occasional bit of saving might occur in a stationary economy, for instance, if there were a once-over change of taste directing demand towards a service requiring more capital than the average. This might entail a once-over but permanent rise in the rate of interest and a once-over readjustment in the prices of goods and factors throughout the system. In the new equilibrium there might be more capital in existence, but the rate of saving per annum would once again be zero.

A further modification of the assumptions may be possible and desirable still within the framework of Statics. If one allows once-over changes in taste, why not once-over changes in the supply schedules of one or other of the factors? A once-over emigration of labour or increase of capital or improvement in an export market or even a technological invention may still be catered for by the static principles, with a consequent readjustment of values and quantities throughout the system, the economy again settling down to a new equilibrium when the once-over injection has been assimilated. But postulate a continuing stream of new inventions, a continuing change of taste, moving always in the direction of services requiring capital above the previous average, or a continuing increase of capital available at a given rate of interest, and then we are in a dynamic economy and the static equations will not alone suffice to solve our problems.

Of the three variables which I have mentioned, two may, as a first approximation, be regarded as independent, namely the size of the population and its productivity per head, and the other as in part at least dependent, namely the quantity of capital.[1] This is in flat contradiction, of course, to the old classical system. For the time being we may neglect problems connected with risk-bearing.

First we may ask this question, what behaviour of capital is required to be consistent with growth in the

[1] Account is, however, taken in the proper place that the quantity of capital becoming available may affect productivity.

21

other elements, *on the hypothesis that the rate of interest does not change?*

First consider a steady geometric increase in the population, with technical knowledge remaining constant. With interest constant the requirement for capital will grow at the same rate as the population. This requirement will be met if the population steadily saves a constant fraction of its total income. How large this fraction must be depends on the ratio of the value of all capital in use to the value of income during a period.

If there is no technological advance and the rate of interest does not alter, the ratio of the value of capital in use to income per period, which we may call the capital coefficient, will remain constant. I am not considering for the moment what will happen if the requisite fraction of income is not saved, but what saving is requisite to be consistent with a certain type of progress, if the rate of interest does not change.

The requisite fraction of income is equal to the increase of population in a period regarded as a fraction of the whole population multiplied by the capital coefficient. This value is independent of the period chosen, since the length of the period multiplies the population increase while it divides the capital coefficient. Thus if outstanding capital is four times national income per annum and the increase of population 1 per cent per annum, the saving required is 4 per cent of income. Constancy in the capital coefficient implies, if the rate of interest is constant, a constant production period.

With a stationary population and a steadily advancing technology we get a similar result. Technological advances may be labour-saving or capital-saving. The correct definition of a neutral advance has been a matter of disagreement, and I believe I am not challenging any

22

firmly established position if I provide my own. I define a neutral advance as one which, at a constant rate of interest, does not disturb the value of the capital co-efficient; it does not alter the length of the production process.

Clearly in a case of this sort there is no question of a correct definition. One's definition should involve a reasonable use of language. As well as being almost essential as a tool for the kind of approach to the dynamic problem which I am attempting, there is much to be said for my definition both on logical and econometrical grounds. It implies, to put it roughly, that the productivity of labour embodied in machines is raised in equal measure with that of those engaged on minding machines; it implies an equal rise of productivity on the part of all labour however far back or forward it may be between the inception and the final stage in production. No one invention is likely, of course, to have this character, but the sum of inventions occurring in a unit period might well have.

A stream of inventions, which are neutral as defined, will, provided that the rate of interest is unchanged, leave the distribution of the total national product as between labour (in the broadest sense) and capital unchanged. The prevailing character of inventions through a period, in which there is no cumulative change in the rate of interest, can be measured by comparing the growth in the value of capital with the growth of income. This can also be done in each industry separately and in each firm.

It should be noticed in passing that the degree of capitalization of any industry must be tested by the ratio of the interest charge (which may be taken as proportional to the value of its real assets) to its turnover. This is quite different from the ratio of the overhead charges on account

23 C

of capital, viz. interest plus amortization, to turnover. A growth in the second-mentioned ratio does not imply a growth in the first mentioned. For instance, a firm may substitute machinery worth £50,000 and calculated to last five years for machinery worth £50,000 calculated to last twenty to get a given volume of output. Such a substitution might have the appearance of intensifying mechanization, the new machinery taking charge of processes that were formerly done by hand; it would raise the charges due in respect of capital; and it would increase the value of the firm's orders to makers of producers' goods. But it would not involve a higher degree of capitalization, nor would it give rise to any demand for fresh savings. It is important to remember that the proportion of resources in a country devoted to the production of more or less fixed producers' goods for the home market is no index of the degree of capitalization of industry; an increase in the ratio of industries making capital goods to those making consumers' goods need not involve any demand for new savings.

In his *Theory of Wages* Mr. Hicks supplied a somewhat different definition of a neutral invention (pp. 121-127). He defined it as one which raises the marginal productivity of labour and capital in equal proportions. This commends itself to reason, but there are a number of causes which make it unsuitable for my purpose. The special characters of my definition may be brought out by a comparison with his.

1. The Hicks definition makes the neutrality of an invention depend on various elasticities, namely elasticities of substitution as between capital and labour in other industries and of the demand for other products using them in various proportions, throughout the whole economy. Thus the neutrality of the invention depends

24

on circumstances quite unrelated to the intrinsic character of the invention itself. My definition determines the matter solely by reference to the invention itself, and is, on this account, a handier tool in a first approach to a great field of study, in which the utmost simplicity is desirable.

2. Mr. Hicks compares his definition with an earlier one given by Professor Pigou.[1] Pigou's definition makes neutrality depend on what happens on the assumption that the quantities of capital and labour available to the economy are unaffected by the invention. Professor Pigou proceeds to consider, from the point of view of the wider question of the harmony between the interests of " labour " and society as a whole, what will result if the supply of the factors is altered in consequence ; but this analysis is not taken to modify the definition. Mr. Hicks seems to leave the question what is to be assumed about the supply of the factors open. But whether he is taken to follow Professor Pigou in assuming absolutely inelastic supply or not, the position is equally unsatisfactory.

To assume an absolutely inelastic supply in every case is somewhat unrealistic. To allow, on the other hand, that the actual elasticities of supply, whatever they may be from time to time, must be taken into account in determining whether an invention is neutral or not, again makes the definition of neutrality depend not on the intrinsic nature of the invention but on quite outside factors.

Furthermore either assumption and indeed this whole method of approach are quite appropriate in relation to a once-over invention (static analysis), but not to a stream of successive new inventions continuing through time.

In the static scheme of thought it is proper to assume determinate supply schedules of the factors and to conceive

[1] *Economics of Welfare* (2nd edition), pp. 632-638.

of marginal productivities as governed by the intersection of supply and demand curves. A once-over invention leads to a once-over change of price which determines and is determined by a once-over charge in the supply of factors in the ordinary way, the supply schedules being conceived to remain unchanged.

When we have to consider a stream of new inventions confronting a growth of capital (viz. positive saving continuing to accrue) a different technique is required. We must remember that the equilibrating force may not be, as in the static analysis, a price (or set of prices), but a certain rate of change of price.

3. In selecting an assumption for the purpose of defining neutrality one has to choose between the assumption of a fixed supply of factors or that of an increasing one. The assumption of a constant supply schedule of the old-fashioned kind is inappropriate, since that is related to a one-over price charge, which has no significance in dynamics; to put it differently, one co-ordinate of the schedule is a price and not, as is required in dynamics, a rate of change of price.

To assume a constant supply of the factors through time is highly unrealistic in relation to any of the economies in which we are interested, and at the same time sets a much more complicated problem for the definition of neutrality. Thus it may be rejected on two excellent grounds.

As I have chosen to approach the dynamic problem by asking what rate of increase of capital would be consistent with certain rates of increase in other parts of the system, it has seemed simplest to define a neutral stream of inventions as one which shall require a rate of increase of capital equal to the rate of increase of income engendered by it. If the stream of inventions requires capital to increase at a greater rate, then it is labour-saving or capital requiring; and conversely. The rate of interest is assumed to be constant, since that is a simpler assumption than that of a changing rate of interest.

4. The neutrality of an invention would be determined on my definition by reference to what happens to the capital coefficient, if the rate of interest is constant. In the language of Statics this implies an infinitely elastic supply of capital at the existing rate of interest. My definition does not, of course, assume that the supply is infinitely elastic; but if it is, then it will be possible to use it to classify all and sundry inventions as they occur. Those who follow Keynes in holding that, save in conditions of Full Employment, the supply of capital is in fact infinitely elastic at a given rate of interest, should give my definition a particularly good mark for its econometric soundness.

5. It does not appear possible to say whether Mr. Hicks's definition or mine would put more actual inventions into the labour-saving box. His depends partly on the outside circumstances, mine on the intrinsic character of the invention only. I cannot find any consideration making it probable that either his or mine would put more in.

I hope, I may say in digression, already to be giving you a dim conception—and I only conceive dimly myself—of the kind of revolution that is required in economics. I want to see those keen tools of thought of Pigou and Hicks, which have been so finely used to perfect static theory, applied to the rough dynamics of Ricardo, changing it indeed out of recognition in the process, as modern marginal analysis has already long since changed the theories of price and cost of Adam Smith and Ricardo. This should involve a considerable re-writing of economics.

But I do not share the views of those who hold that, in place of the old theory, we are to have a brand new kind of economics, chapter one of which is to be a definition of the National Income and chapter two—goodness knows what.

It must not be taken to be implied that a neutral invention as defined is the most likely kind of invention. Nothing of this sort is presupposed in my definition or for that matter in the definitions advanced by others. I might be permitted to observe in passing, however, that it is not my impression that in recent years inventions have been predominantly of a character tending to raise the capital coefficient as calculated at and determined by a constant rate of interest; it is not my impression that inventions have been predominantly labour-saving in the sense defined.

With a stationary population, then, and a steady and neutral technological advance, the new capital required would be a constant fraction of income equal to the increase of income (or output) in any period considered as a fraction of total income multiplied by the capital coefficient. The same period must be used in calculating the increase of output and in computing the capital coefficient.

If a is the fraction of income required to be saved when population is increasing at a given rate X and technology is stationary and b the fraction of income required to be saved when population is stationary and technological advance makes possible an increase of output at rate Y, then, when there is both a population increase of X and an increase of output per head of Y, the fraction of income required to be saved will be $a + b + ab$. ab is likely to be a very small quantity and may be safely neglected.

The foregoing analysis implied that a constant value

means a constant power of purchasing goods. I have nothing new to say about index numbers! There have always been economists, however, from Ricardo to Mr. Hawtrey, who have preferred a labour measure of value.

I do not share this preference. We are not likely in the foreseeable future, assuming that totalitarianism will not triumph, to have a labour measure of value. It implies that the average of money rewards paid to workers never rises, any increases in some part of the field being offset by equivalent decreases in others. This is an awkward programme; decreases are never welcome; it is easier to allow sectional increases to stand and accept a gradual rise in the over-all average of money rewards. Provided this rise did not proceed more quickly than the increase of average output per head, the consequent system would be sufficiently stable. Furthermore the pleasure given by an occasional increase of money income is probably somewhat greater than that given by an equivalent fall in the prices of purchasable goods and services. Is it not a little sadistic to seek to deprive men of this increment of pleasure, for the sake of—what? — a mere academic preference.

Again, it seems that the labour measure would accord too much to the dead hand of the past. When a contract is made for a future payment in money, it is certainly implied or hoped that the future money will have as good a power of purchasing goods as present money. But it is not, I think, implied that future money will purchase the same fraction of the national output per head as present money.

One reason for the preference for the labour measure may be due to a sense of the inherent difficulties in framing a satisfactory index number of prices to be a yardstick for testing the goods value of money. It must be remembered, however, that this problem of an index number is not eliminated by the labour measure. There are various kinds of labour, and a labour index number would be as necessary as a goods index number. That index number would not only have to include the various trades and grades of work but also such labour as that of the judge, the surgeon and the general manager. Would this number really be so very much easier to compute?

None the less this preference is so influential that it is desirable to remark once and for all on its bearing upon the relations that have been set out. In the case of an economy stationary in numbers but making neutral technological progress with a constant rate of interest, no new saving would be required. The labour value of the total of capital assets would remain constant, although its goods value would rise at the same rate as national income.

This lack of any requirement for savings in the circumstances assumed is a rather notable fact, worth pausing to reflect upon, since our own economy is one in which the population will not increase in the middle-distance future, but in which we hope that national income will increase. If there is likely to be any tendency towards a redundancy of savings in this country — and we must also keep our eyes upon the United States — then the fact that a labour measure of value would render *all* saving in the circumstances supposed superfluous must be deemed to have some bearing on the desirability of that measure.

It might be argued that, since what savers want is disposable capital or income in future, and since, on a labour standard, existing titles or assets would appreciate in terms of goods both as regards their capital value and the income due from them, private people would, so to speak, find their saving automatically done for them, and would no longer find it desirable to set aside any part of their income for this purpose. While this argument may have some force, it does not go the whole way. It supposes prescience as regards the continued maintenance of the labour standard. Furthermore many would-be savers are not already owners of titles or assets or not in sufficient quantity to satisfy their prospective requirements; these would continue to save in the ordinary way despite the labour standard. Logically, it might be argued, the saving on the part of those desiring to build up their position at a greater rate than the national average should be offset by dis-saving by others. Arguing that their titles or assets would secure them a rising goods income over and above the level that on a goods standard they would deem it necessary to save for, they should begin living on capital, thus reducing their unwanted future accretions of income in terms of goods. But would they? or would they in all cases? Is there not a certain *vis inertiae* in respect of savings already made in the past? It can surely hardly be doubted that this labour standard would cause savings in the aggregate to be higher than they would be on a goods standard.

The case of companies should also be looked at. On any system these cause savings to be undertaken to an extent that may often exceed what their shareholders would volunteer from private motives. Yet not all company expansion is financed in this way. Debentures, preference shares, ordinary shares are occasionally issued! Under the labour standard the opportunities for this would be almost entirely eliminated. With the progressive fall in prices companies would have to increase the volume of their physical assets steadily without fresh issue. The auditors require that the cash value of the assets be sustained at a level equal to the nominal value of the liabilities.

If this were done in the case of all companies, then the total goods value of their assets would grow as quickly as the total goods value of the whole national capital. This would be the automatic effect of correct accountancy as required by the auditors. Thus there would be no scope whatever for fresh issues of capital, except as an offset to the loss of assets by other companies going bankrupt. Incidentally many more companies would find themselves faced with bankruptcy, which might, however, only mean, given the modern outlook, that many more unsound positions would get bolstered up at the cost of the tax-payer.

I cannot resist the temptation to relate this line of thought to certain proposals by Professor von Hayek which were much discussed some years ago. He advocated a monetary system which would put us in a narrower strait-jacket than the labour standard itself. I may note in passing, however, that since he allowed the monetary authorities to issue additional credit to offset any decline in the velocity of circulation, his system would involve pumping in new money during a depression on a more heroic scale than the most audacious authority has ever undertaken in practice.

Professor von Hayek's scheme would have prices fall not merely in proportion to output per head, but to total national output. Thus, even if there were population growth, no new saving would be required if inventions were neutral and the rate of interest constant. The gist of the foregoing arguments suggests that, since a labour standard, still more a Hayek standard, would undoubtedly tend to cause savings to stand higher than they would otherwise be, the monetary authorities should take the tendency of savings to be redundant or deficient as a prime criterion for inclining them, to the extent that they have the power to influence these things (which depend much more on autonomous changes in wage, salary and fee rates), towards a goods standard in the one case or towards a labour standard in the other. This leads us to a conclusion, somewhat paradoxical, which is the exact opposite of Professor von Hayek's. Given the demand for new capital (depending mainly on the potential rate of growth and the character of inventions), then the greater the disposition of individuals to save voluntarily the more ought the banks to increase the supply of bank credit.

I do not wish to re-enter the old debate. It always appeared to me that it was a cardinal error to suppose that the volume of additional bank credit could simply be added to voluntary saving to assess the total supply of capital available to meet requirements, since the additional bank credit is automatically and precisely offset by new hoarding of equal amount. And if it be objected — ah, but this additional hoarding is unnatural and in some sense forced — one asks, how much of it? Surely some new hoarding is natural in a progressive society? The Hayekians reply that none will be natural or necessary, if only prices fall as they ought to. But, we retort, why ought they to? If they do not, fresh hoarding will be natural and necessary. It soon becomes evident that we are arguing in a circle, that Professor von Hayek's proposition only posed the problem without solving it. Keynes has since advanced a solution with which you may or may not be satisfied. The notion that *any* increase of bank credit supplements voluntary saving does not appear in Wicksell, and I suggest that Professor von Hayek's attempt to improve on Wicksell in this matter has put us on a false scent.

In all the jungle of controversy that followed the publication of Professor von Hayek's views, I do not recollect seeing the point made that a restrictive monetary policy of the kind he advocated would greatly increase the automatic saving by companies in terms of goods values. Yet this may well be the most important objection of all.

In what follows I shall assume a goods standard of value.

So far I have made a first approach to the question of the demand for saving in a growing economy. We must next consider what may be said about its probable supply. I shall crave indulgence in dwelling at some length on this topic, not holding out the hope of very clear-cut results, but because its traditional treatment appears to me gravely defective.

THE SUPPLY OF SAVING

STATISTICAL studies upon how the flow of savings is related to the level of income and other economic aggregates are well under way, and we may look forward to large developments in this field. It should be a most fruitful one for the econometrician's art. I shall not venture into it, but shall confine myself to a brief visit to the more old-fashioned realm of theoretical analysis. Such an investigation may yield assistance to the econometrician, by clarifying concepts and suggesting possible connexions requiring study. What is usually said in the text-books on this subject is unsatisfactory, and the great masters do not appear to have done their best work in this department.

In explaining why savers expect to get and succeed in getting a remuneration for the mere act of waiting — risk apart — economists are apt to lay chief stress on the phenomenon of time preference. The individual who has free choice tends to prefer a given sum of money now to an equal sum at a future date. Time preference in this broad sense is complex and requires analysis.

First it is necessary to be clear what exactly it is that has to be explained. Aristotle and his followers deemed it unnatural that it should be possible to gain an increment of money merely by parting with money for a period, and concluded that it was wrong. If indeed there were no countervailing considerations to justify this accretion, the phenomenon of interest would not merely come up for

35

moral judgment, it would violate the most basic law of economics, namely that one cannot get something for nothing. In any community with a reasonable amount of communication and mutual knowledge, if it appears that something can be bought and then resold at a clear net profit with no risk attached, then the demand for that something will be so stimulated and its price so bidden up that the net profit will be eliminated. This is the process of arbitrage. If gain is to be made by buying silver in New York and simultaneously selling it in London, so that there is profit available without risk, so much will be demanded in New York and so much offered for sale in London that the price spread will immediately be reduced to what is needed to cover the cost of transport.

If £103 can be obtained with certainty on January 1, 1949, in return for £100 now, is this indeed £3 for nothing? Then why would not so much money be offered now against the delivery on January 1, 1949, that the margin of £3 would be eliminated?

The most fundamental principle that has to be adduced in explanation of the phenomenon is the well-known Law of the Diminishing Utility of Income. This Law may be included in the notion of time preference in its broadest sense; but it is necessary to extricate it from the broader concept because it is more fundamental than, and may operate in a different manner from, the other element in time preference, which may be called pure time preference.

We all have some idea of the nature of this pure time preference. We do not see the future so vividly as the present and underrate the advantage of having money at a future date compared with that of having it now. Professor Pigou has referred to our defective " telescopic faculty ".[1]   Also we may be dead at the future date and not rate the welfare of our heirs as highly as our own. The desire to use the money now is reinforced by animal appetite.   Greed may be thought to be as appropriate a name for this attitude as time preference, though less dignified.   Time preference in this sense is a human infirmity, probably stronger in primitive than in civilized man.

No such stigma can be attached to the rejection of £3 " for nothing " if it is based on the principle of Diminishing Utility of Income.   If a man has every reason to suppose that he will have an income of £500 in 1948 and one of £500 in 1949 and no reason to suppose that his needs will be greater in the latter year, he will not gain anything by exchanging £100 in 1948 for £103 in 1949.   On the contrary he will almost certainly lose.   In 1948 he must cut his consumption to £400 for the advantage of raising it to £603 in 1949.   It is true that he will have £1003 to spend in the two years together instead of £1000.   But regard must be paid to the utility of the pounds.   In 1948 he foregoes the pounds numbered from 401 to 500 and in 1949 he acquires pounds numbered from 501 to 603. Each of the former set of pounds is likely to have considerably higher utility than any of the latter, and it is most unlikely that the beggarly extra £3 will compensate for this.   Such a man would probably do himself injury by seeking to get this £3 " for nothing ".   If there are sufficient members of the community in this position the normal process of arbitrage will not eliminate the margin of £3.   The argument is the same as that applied to gambling by Marshall, in this following Bentham, as we are reminded by Dr. Stark ; [2] but Marshall failed to make

[1] *Economics of Welfare* (2nd edition), p. 25.
[2] *Economic Journal*, December 1946, p. 601.

this explicitly the basis of the theory of saving. Yet saving is really a more important instance than gambling of the operation of this principle.

Thus there are two quite distinct reasons for spending now rather than waiting for a larger sum later. One is that the larger sum later may veritably have less utility than the smaller sum now, the other the lack of telescopic faculty whereby we fail to estimate justly the utility that the larger sum will have. It must be noticed that even if we were perfectly enlightened in our attitude to the future, perfectly provident and disinterested, altogether lacking in brute passion and appetite and had a thoroughly adequate telescope for surveying future years, there might none the less be a rate of interest owing to the diminishing utility of income. The rate of interest ruling is by no means a measure of the extent to which people discount future satisfactions compared with present. Many textbooks leave the opposite impression on the reader's mind. I think that Marshall does so in his *Principles* (p. 122). It is true that he characteristically adds all the necessary qualifications to make his statement formally correct and amplifies them in a footnote. The text runs as follows:

We can however get an artificial measure of the rate at which he discounts future benefits by making two assumptions. These are, firstly, that he expects to be about as rich at the future date as he is now; and secondly, that his capacity for deriving benefit from the things which money will buy will on the whole remain unchanged, though it may have increased in some directions and diminished in others. On these assumptions, if he is willing, but only just willing, to spare a pound from his expenditure now, with the certainty of having (for the disposal of himself or his heirs) a guinea one year hence, we may fairly say that he discounts future benefits that are perfectly secure (subject only to conditions of human mortality) at the rate of 5 per cent per annum. And on these assumptions the rate at which he discounts future (certain) benefits, will be the rate at which he can discount money in the money market.

How many would perceive clearly, after reading this, that there may well be a rate of interest even if no one discounts future satisfactions at all? It is really a masterpiece in the art of converting an ancient fallacy into a truth in a way that conceals that the ancient fallacy has been altered. I suspect that Marshall wanted to reiterate that the rate of interest reflected the time discount, because economists had usually said so, out of his loving care to preserve the continuity of the subject. What is really required is to bring out the fallacy in that ancient formulation.

Some purists may prefer not to break down the broader concept of time preference into its constituent elements on the ground that economists should confine their attention to market facts, such as the actual swap of £100 for £103, and not look below the surface for motives. It is enough to know, they would argue, that people do prefer £100 now to £102 a year hence; that is an objective ascertainable fact; once we begin peering into the reasons why, which cannot be measured or demonstrated, we shall be lost in a maze of conjecture and forfeit our character of scientists dealing with quantitative data. In certain instances such a maxim may be wise; but it must not be elevated into an absolute and universal principle in economics. It is the economist's business to examine the relation between procedure and objectives, and definitions of the latter must to some extent depend on introspection. Introspectively the two motives for not saving can be quite clearly distinguished generally, although it does not follow that their respective force can be measured in each particular case. The diminishing utility of income is a principle adequately based on the observation that identical physical objects, which have utility, do not have the same degree of utility on every occasion of use; and in particular cases it may be perfectly clear that a man does not choose to save because the cut in his present consumption would be so painful as not to be balanced by the available accretion of income later. On the other hand, Professor Pigou's defective telescopic faculty is also a clear concept; examples of palpable improvidence can easily be picked up. There are two reasons why it is important to draw the distinction.[1]

I said that the Law of Diminishing Utility was more fundamental than pure time preference. It has a wider application—for instance to a planned regime in which the volume of saving is fixed by a benevolent government. After all, pure time preference is a weakness; a man may choose to sacrifice 2 units of utility — of utility not money — in 20 years from now for the sake of 1 unit now; but in 20 years' time he will presumably regret having done so. Unfortunately he will not then be able to reverse the process. On the assumption — unwarranted, no doubt, some of you may think — that a government is capable of planning what is best for its subjects, it will pay no attention to pure time preference, a polite expression for rapacity and the conquest of reason by passion. But it must certainly pay attention to the Law of Diminishing Utility of Income. Perhaps the U.S.S.R. did not do so sufficiently in the first Five-Year Plan, though from the security point of view its ruthless saving turned out well. Sir Hubert Henderson, in a notable passage which does full justice to the importance of the Law of Diminishing

---

[1] The distinction is sharply drawn in F. P. Ramsey's well-known article in the *Economic Journal* (December 1928).

Utility in this connexion, has suggested that the unequal distribution of income in Britain in the hungry 'forties may have caused saving to proceed at a pace that was too rapid from the point of view of the economic welfare of the country considered over a long term.[1] And now at this moment we are living in a regime in which the volume of national saving is largely controlled by the government. Is it also, perhaps, pushing on too quickly? If there is to be a war within ten years it will have proved wise whatever the present cost. On the other hand the consequent prolonged oppression of the consumer, who has already had so much to suffer during a decade and may suffer permanent psychological injury by unnecessary and apparently unending austerity, and the danger that the country in its infatuation for capital outlay may fail in consequence to balance its external accounts in time to redeem its honour, are very weighty considerations on the other side.

Secondly, Diminishing Utility and pure time preference operate in a different manner as forces restricting saving, and will be differently affected by changes in the rate of interest or other relevant circumstances. In future I shall refer to pure time preference simply as time preference.

The fundamental theory of the supply of saving may be set out in the form of equations. Let C_1 stand for consumption, viz. income less saving, in year one and C_r stand for consumption in another year, year r. Let e stand for the average elasticity of the income utility curve over the relevant range. Let T stand for the amount of utility now which is equally preferred with one unit of utility a year later; thus if the rate of time discount per annum were 5 per cent, T would be $\frac{100}{105}$. Let R be the number

[1] *Supply and Demand*, pp. 131-132.

of pounds to which £1 accumulates at the end of the year at the current rate of interest; thus at 3 per cent $R = 1\cdot03$. The following equation assumes that needs are expected to be the same in year r as in year 1. An adjustment for variation of need involves, however, no difficulty of principle, and can readily be made by multiplying C_r by a coefficient expressing the magnitude of expected total needs in year r compared with those in year 1. Then

$$C_1 = C_r \left(1 - e \left\{ 1 - \frac{1}{T'R'} \right\} \right).$$

A similar equation may be written to relate the present year to each future year. If we had only to consider a finite number of future years until some foreseen time at which the globe would be vaporized by a nuclear explosion, say n years, then we should have $(n-1)$ equations of the above type, together with one further identical equation expressing the fact that in the period as a whole income must be equal to consumption. Let Y_r stand for income in year r from all sources except interest on, and return of, past savings made within the period. Then the identical equation is as follows:

$$(C_1 + ... + C_n) - (Y_1 + ... + Y_n)$$
$$= (Y_1 - C_1)R^{n-1} + ... + (Y_n - C_n)R^o.$$

I shall return to the problem of infinity presently.

These equations can be used in various ways. On the one hand one may assume in theory that a man knows his own mind and is able to evaluate e and T for himself. The equations would tell him how, in the light of this knowledge, he should plan his expenditure. In practice, of course, the ideas of people about their own satisfactions and futures are far too vague to be given numerical expression. None the less the equations may be taken to represent a tendency. By inserting probable values for e and T we can deduce what effects changes in the rate of interest or in other relevant circumstances are likely to have on the flow of saving. I have used the equations with some labour for this purpose with results which I shall presently expound.

Alternatively it might be possible to use the equations for an inverse process. By accumulating observations of the values of C_1, C_2, C_3, etc., it might be possible, R of course being known, to deduce the values of e and T. If the equations could be solved in this manner it would give a hard objective justification for discriminating, in the way I have insisted on, between the influence of the diminishing utility of income and that of time preference.

It ought to be possible to get some approximate valuation of e for various levels of income independently. Thus if it is found that a rise of piece rates causes a man to work less hard, we can infer that for him over the relevant range $e < 1$. Such a finding should not surprise us. The idea that, in order to impose on a man unaltered sacrifice as his income alters, progressive rather than proportional taxation is required — I put the matter in this way to avoid interpersonal comparison — implies that $e < 1$.

By experiment it should be possible to determine e more precisely. Could not a combination of managers and shop stewards be found who were sufficiently interested in basic principles to conduct such a series of experiments? They would not, of course, be easy! Let a standard rate of wage be paid for part of the normal day and a bonus at a different rate for the residue. The individual must have complete freedom to vary the number of hours worked over and above those for which the standard rate was paid. We should begin with a certain standard rate and a certain rate of bonus, together amounting to a basic minimum wage, and so arranged that the representative individual chose to work, say, an eight-hour day, neither more nor less. Then a rise of wages should be inaugurated by gradual stages. The standard rate and the bonus rate would both have to be altered at each stage, probably in different proportions, in such wise that the earner of his own free will still chose to work eight hours. This double variation designed to keep the man voluntarily working eight hours is required in order to give a fixed yardstick with which to measure the marginal utility of income. This yardstick would be the disutility of the eighth hour — or four hundred and eightieth minute — of a particular kind of labour. The elasticity of the marginal utility of income would be measured by the proportionate rise in the total wage paid per day divided by the proportionate rise of the *rate* of bonus payment.

The theory of saving which I have advanced implies that a man makes a conspectus of his probable income and needs for all future years. This is not altogether unrealistic, if we confine his consideration to his probable lifetime. Out of the mists of uncertainty through which a man views his future, some basic facts begin to emerge, such as that he ought to save for a pension or the support of children, or that his prospects of earning are such and such. The uncertainties will always be very great. A theory of saving will give but the roughest approximation; it·may, however, reliably be used to show certain tendencies.

In view of the theoretical difficulties inherent in the subject, it may be well, as an approximate approach, to divide an individual's savings into two parts : (i) those required to satisfy his own needs during his life, and (ii) those intended to be passed on. In practice men do not make this distinction at all sharply; none the less it may serve to analyse the bundle of motives, some semi-conscious, that determine his behaviour. Corporate saving must also be considered.

The amount of saving that a man does for his own sake ((i) above) is determined by such factors as his expectation of increasing income, of increasing needs and of his probable inability to earn income in the last phase. To some extent the first and second of these may balance and pension provision may be the dominating motive. If he does not seek to make his pension as large as his income when at work, this need not be due to time preference, but to a just recognition that an elderly person's needs may be less than those of a man in his prime of life. If a man had no time preference, he should redistribute consumption through time so as to make it increase (in relation to his needs) at a rate which made its marginal utility fall at a rate equal to the rate of interest. With zero interest he would keep its amount in relation to his needs, and thereby its marginal utility, constant. If he has a time preference he will make it rise (or fall) so that the marginal utility in year r is $\dfrac{1}{R^r T^r}$ times its marginal utility in year 1. The equations I have set out express this. They may be used to analyse probable provision by saving for a man's life, his probable expectation of life being represented by n. In analysing provision for heirs we must probably be content with vaguer considerations.

In a society in which population and the state of technology are stationary, saving of the former category should be zero. Members of each generation will save for themselves, but the older members of the population will be simultaneously dis-saving an equal amount.

45

It is not so clear that saving for heirs (ii) will also be zero, save, perhaps, after the lapse of a very long time, which it is unrealistic even in this schematic exercise to consider. It would be wrong to suppose that in a society otherwise stationary and expected to remain so, no saving would occur on the ground that, since one's heirs are expected to have as good an income as one's own, there would be no gain of utility from transferring an additional power of consumption to them. It may be expedient to provide something for the earlier part of their lives, in which dis-saving at the expense of their own later years may be technically difficult. It is not certain whether a particular heir will have the capacity to earn as much as his father. It is useful to provide in advance against unknown contingencies which may befall him. So long as there is some positive interest, there may be a gain of utility even although the heir can in fact steadily earn as much as his father — in other words the motive making for saving represented in our equations still applies in some degree to saving for heirs, although no doubt with diminished force. Furthermore an unearned income is an amenity, allowing freedom of manœuvre, freedom, if desired, to devote one's life to good, although uneconomic, ends. For all these reasons a father may be disposed to sacrifice certain present utilities in order to add to the sum that can be handed on. It is a mistake to suppose that, in a stationary society, all these things will already have been thought of, so that the present generation need do no more than pass on the inherited wealth it has received. The amenities in question may be deemed to exceed, pound for pound, the utility of some small part of present income but not that of a larger part. Thus it might take very many generations of a stationary society to provide all the amenities, which might be deemed to justify some saving. The amount of saving would presumably tend to fall in each generation.

In such a society there would be no demand for saving at all at a constant rate of interest. Thus it would be necessary to have a falling rate of interest to give employment to the savings volunteered.

There remains the question of corporate saving. This cannot be regarded as a third sector of saving that has to be added to the two classes of personal saving in assessing total saving. Its distinguishing feature is its motive. Under personal saving we have considered the desire to rearrange the stream of income in a more advantageous way and to provide against the contingencies of private life. Corporate saving, with which must be grouped some saving by producers working on their own account, is mainly actuated by the desire of entrepreneurs to provide resources for the expansion of business without forfeiting a controlling interest or unduly enlarging fixed charges. But while the motive for this kind of saving is different, the result is that individuals, shareholders or entrepreneurs, are provided with additional capital resources, which may serve to meet their private needs as already classified. For this reason corporate saving may not be additional to personal saving, but part of it. To the extent that the value of a man's business holdings grows, he is exempted from the necessity of saving out of his personal income in order to provide for his private contingencies. It does not follow that corporate saving can be neglected as a separate constituent in total saving. For instance, it is conceivable that corporate saving might exceed the total that all individuals would be disposed to save for private convenience. What is much more probable is that owing to *vis inertiae* or business ambition many individuals may be led on by their corporate holdings or business interests to save more than they would choose to, merely in order to provide for their private needs. I shall call an excess of this sort surplus corporate saving; we must add it to personal savings as determined by the fundamental private motives we have examined in order to reach the total saving by the community.

In a stationary society net corporate saving would normally be zero, although particular firms may make positive corporate savings to an extent sufficient to offset losses incurred by others.

Where, however, population and technology are stationary, but individuals are continuing to save in order to increase what is passed on from generation to generation, a fall in the rate of interest is required. In so far as this fall stimulates more roundabout methods of production — and this is the only way in which the fresh savings by individuals can be utilized — it will tend to stimulate corporate saving and thereby surplus corporate saving. When more roundabout methods of production become profitable owing to the fall in interest rates, firms may wish to finance them out of their own resources. This desire is likely to add to the total saving of the community. And this in turn will make it necessary for the rate of interest to fall at a greater rate, if a steady advance is to be maintained. I shall have presently to ask you to examine very closely this notion of the rate of interest falling continuously at an appropriate rate.

Thus with population and technology stationary, there might well, in a prosperous and secure society, be a factor of increase at work for a very long period. If all went well, methods of production would get steadily more roundabout.

It may be convenient here to consider the likely effect

of a falling rate of interest on the supply of saving. Unhappily it does not seem possible to give a definite answer. We have already seen that a falling rate of interest is likely to evoke a stream of corporate saving that would not otherwise take place. In the sector of saving for posterity, it does not seem possible to make any guess at all. Cassel has urged that saving of this kind would be likely to fall off sharply when the rate of interest fell below a certain critical point; but his argument is very impressionistic, and it does not seem that much can be built upon it. There remains the saving required to provide for the saver's needs during his own life-time, saving destined to be subsequently dissipated in dis-saving. I shall call this hump-saving. Is a falling rate of interest likely to cause the size of the hump to shrink?

I have considered this problem in the light of the equations, giving e, T and R a wide range of values within the bounds of probability. In every case it seems that saving will be less with a lower rate of interest. Marshall says rather dogmatically that saving may be expected to respond positively to higher interest rates; it is possible that he secretly made similar calculations to mine! His dogmatism is not usually followed in more recent text-books.

My results are rather surprisingly decisive, surprisingly because my model is that of a man saving during early and middle life in order to buy a life annuity on retirement — future contingencies other than a retirement pension within the saver's life can conveniently be subsumed under the pension — and it is precisely in this kind of case that it is popularly supposed that a high rate of interest is likely to reduce saving. I suspect that this popular view arises from neglect of compound interest, the fact that with a high interest yield there is more accrued interest available to be re-saved. In many of the cases I have analysed, a higher rate of interest reduces the cut in consumption which the individual is induced to make in his early years, and enables him to sustain consumption at a higher level in all years; none the less in all these cases he does more saving altogether during his life.

It may be that those who claim that a fall in the rate of interest will increase saving are thinking only of its immediate effect, and I can confirm their view in the sense that it would theoretically in certain cases cause a larger immediate cut in consumption. Yet it is doubtful if there is much validity even in the notion that the immediate effect of a fall in interest would be to increase saving. For in the case of this deliberate hump-saving, a man will tend to work to some rather extensive plan, and is not likely to readjust his ideas immediately when a change in the rate of interest takes place.

Furthermore, the popular analysis works in terms of a once-over reduction in the rate of interest. When the fall is continuous, there is no distinction between an immediate effect and a later effect. The hump of savings at any time embodies the savings of people of all ages; it is a cross section of the near and distant effects of the falling rate. Thus we need only have regard to the total effect of a falling rate upon hump-saving, the distinction between the near and more distant effect disappearing. If a lower rate entails a smaller hump on the part of those influenced by it, a continuously falling rate will be synchronously accompanied by a fall in the size of the total hump at a rate that is determined by the total effect of the falling interest. No doubt accelerations and decelerations ought also to be considered, but I will not attempt in this introductory essay in dynamics to deal with them. There will also be a disposition to ask what happens when there is a change in the rate of fall or in the acceleration of fall, when there is a kink in the curve. This probably represents the urge in the breast of the expert on economic statics to get back to familiar ground, since kinks can probably best be dealt with by the methods of statical analysis. Therefore I eschew that question in this context.

We are very much in the dark as to the value of e. In my calculations I have made alternative assumptions, giving it values between 0 and 1. For T I have assumed values between 1 (no time preference) and a value somewhat above ·96. The latter represents a rather strong time preference, since it means that a man would reckon one unit of present utility (not of income) at the beginning of his working life as equal to no less than 4 units of utility (not of income) 40 years later.

It seems that saving is much more responsive to changes in the rate of interest if e is high; it also appears that it is somewhat more responsive if T is low, that is if Time Preference is strong.

The upshot of this analysis is indecisive. Surplus corporate savings are likely to rise in response to a falling rate of interest while hump-savings are likely to fall; the effect on saving for posterity is unknown.

What happens if we introduce other factors of increase? If population increases, while technology is stationary, it appears that the hump sector of capital accumulation is likely to increase at the same rate as the population. The hump sector is the sum of all the capitals intended to be dissipated by individuals now living; in a stationary population this dissipation would be exactly balanced by the hump-savings of the younger people. In a steadily growing population the number of humps is being increased, and therefore the size of the sum of all humps is growing at the same rate as the population itself. Thus hump-accumulations will increase at such a rate that if the other sectors of accumulation increased at the same rate, the demand for new capital would be precisely met at a constant rate of interest.

In this case, as in all cases, corporate saving may be expected to vary with requirements and consequently to become positive if population is increasing by an amount which bears the same ratio to existing corporate accumulations that the increment of population bears to the existing population. There may be some rough presumption, therefore, that the sector of total saving constituted by new surplus corporate saving will be positive, and keep a steady relation to the new hump-saving and the increment of population.

What of saving for posterity? Are the accumulations passed on likely to grow as quickly as the population? This might prove a severe strain on a population whose income per head was not growing. It must be remembered that the more rapid the growth of population, the more deeply the existing population would have to cut into its standard of living in order to achieve this target for its successors. Such achievement need not be ruled out; indeed the target might be exceeded. Much would no doubt depend on the level of wealth achieved by the community, on how near to animal appetites were the utilities that had to be sacrificed in order to provide successors with these amenities.

It seems that only if each generation adds to the corpus of inherited wealth enough to allow each member of the next generation to inherit as much on average as each member of the preceding one, will the total saving of the community be sufficient to provide for all capital requirements at a constant rate of interest.

It is at least clear from the comparison of the stationary population with the increasing one, that an accumulation requiring a falling rate of interest is much more likely in the former case. In that case no new capital at all is required with interest constant while some increase in average estates passing at death is almost certain, so that with interest unchanged we could confidently expect a redundancy of saving. In the other case it is not clear whether such a redundancy is even probable.

Finally, we have to consider increasing output per head. Once again corporate saving and surplus corporate saving are likely to respond positively to the extra requirements due to technical advance.

If we assume e and T to be constant as income rises, hump-saving is likely to increase in proportion to income and therefore to requirements. But e and T are not likely to remain constant. As regards e I believe that we are entirely in the dark. I know of no pointers whatever. It is sometimes assumed, I believe, that e is lower for high incomes, but I regard this as entirely without foundation. The requirement for progressive taxation is not that e should fall as income rises, but only that it should be below one. A low value of e is inimical to saving.

On the other hand there seems to be a presumption that time preference will fall (that T will increase). As income rises our consumption is less dominated by basic physical need and becomes more amenable to rational planning. We " look before and after " more frequently. A strong time preference is indicative of a low degree of civilization. Thus it is proper to assume a rise in T with rising income per head, and this would involve the aggregate of hump-saving increasing more rapidly than income. This may well prove to be a point of central importance in the evolution of our economy.

As against this it might be said that if a representative man foresaw the prospect of a rising income in his lifetime, not merely owing to his own relative advancement which he might expect in any case, but owing to the general advance of the community, this should reduce his need to accumulate in order to cover his own future contingencies. We are here, however, pitting the force of an expectation of increase against that of an actual increase. *A priori* one would expect the former to be weaker. But there is a more fundamental objection to this line of argument.

It is one dimension out and well illustrates the dangers besetting the novice in economic dynamics. Whatever force an expectation of the general advancement of the community and thereby in a man's own circumstances may have in making him think it unnecessary to provide so large a reserve to meet future contingencies, it has no effect whatever on the rate of growth in the size of humps. It is only an increase in the amount of advancement expected that would have the effect of tending to reduce the size of humps. On the assumption that expectations correspond to the facts expected, it is only an acceleration of growth and not a growth itself in average income per head that would tend to reduce the rate of hump accumulation. In this tentative treatment I am not dealing with accelerations. In a boom an acceleration of this kind may play some part — there comes into the heads of many the idea " we seem to be getting rich so quickly ; why bother? ", so that their normal canons of providence are by degrees temporarily undermined. Such a process would increase the vicious spiral effect of boom. I doubt, however, if much that is important will be missed by neglect of longer period accelerations.

So far as hump accumulations are concerned, therefore,

a rise of income per head is likely to cause them to grow at a greater rate than income.

What, finally, is the effect of a rising income per head on saving for posterity? We saw that if income per head were stationary, there would be likely to be a tendency for the rate of increase in the size of average legacies to decline, as more and more amenities could be secured for children by merely passing on to children inherited capital intact; amenities of less and less importance would have to be pitted against the same marginal utility of a constant income. But with income per head rising this principle would no longer operate. It is true that as time went on and average legacies increased, further additions would provide less important amenities for children; on the other hand, since actual incomes were continuing to rise, the sacrifices required to provide those extra amenities would also be declining. All would depend on the comparative elasticities of the own income curve and the amenities for children curve. Nothing very definite can be said ; it is not unreasonable to suppose that the average size of legacies might increase at the same rate as average income per head.

There is a consideration, however, which suggests that average amounts passing at death might rise more rapidly than income per head. Time preference is relevant here too. The same force that we may expect to make hump accumulation grow more quickly than income per head — the increasing disposition to look ahead — may well affect provision for children also, and in the same way. The richer man has more mental energy to devote to thinking about the future.

I shall not attempt to deal with the incidence and indirect effects of taxation.

I fear that the result of this rather lengthy analysis is

somewhat inconclusive. One negative conclusion stands out. There seems to be no broad presumption that the rate of saving will be precisely what is required to sustain a steady advance of production with the rate of interest constant. We may have to contemplate a continuously rising or falling rate of interest, and that will prove to be a matter of great moment.

On the positive side it appears clear that a stationary or declining population is more likely to require a falling rate of interest than an increasing one. This already appeared in the crude dynamics of Adam Smith. Furthermore it seems probable that, in a stationary population with income per head advancing, the accumulations volunteered would increase more rapidly than income, or, therefore, than requirements, save in so far as those were enlarged by capital-requiring inventions. This appears almost certain in the sector that has been called hump accumulation. In the case of accumulation for posterity the presumption is less strong. The possibility of a flow of total saving requiring a falling rate of interest, especially in a stationary population, is certainly one that cannot be neglected.

It should not be difficult to amass statistical information in order to throw light on these relations. Evaluations of total income and income per head and of total capital are proceeding apace. The relation between the growth of total capital and the growth of capital passing at death — before and after deduction of death duties — needs attention, since this should bring out the relation between hump-saving and saving for posterity. One great pitfall must, however, be noticed. All that has been said relates to the propensity to save; it has been seen that continuing changes in interest rates may be needed to absorb the supply. I will not anticipate matters now by considering

Keynes's theories of the unresponsiveness of the rate of interest. Suffice it to say that my analysis has been concerned with mutual relations in an economy advancing at its potentially optimum rate. Clearly not all economies have so advanced. It is not only a question of the disturbance of the trade cycle, but also since 1920, if not before, and more markedly since 1929 — in fact in the period in which fullest statistical information is available — there is the question of a chronic tendency to depression. This must have a distorting effect on the relations I have set out, and the statistics must be interpreted with this in mind.

There is one matter that I have not so far mentioned, which has a rather important bearing on the relations discussed — namely the dead-weight debt. Capital requirements have been considered by reference to the growth of capital called for by a growth of income. The rate at which capital requirements may grow in various circumstances has been compared with the rate at which individuals (and companies) may seek to add to their accumulations. But from the point of view of savers — though not of the users of savings — accumulations to date include the dead-weight debt. If the dead-weight debt is small this may be of no great moment. In Britain at present the national debt is of preponderating importance and of an order of magnitude comparable to the whole real capital of the nation. Take a simple case, in which income and capital requirements are growing at the rate of 2 per cent per annum and individuals and companies are disposed to increase their capital accumulations at the rate of 2 per cent per annum also. This would seem to be a most harmonious state of affairs in which the rate of interest might remain constant. But if half of existing capital holdings consisted of dead-weight debt the disposition of individuals to add to their capital at the rate of 2 per cent per annum would provide industry with twice the capital it needed.

It may be argued that the artificially stimulated build up of dead-weight debt during a war should greatly reduce the propensity to save thereafter. This is more likely to be the case in Britain after World War II in which artificial savings were more widely diffused than after World War I when they were more concentrated in the hands of profiteers. It may be that, in consequence of this surfeit of saving, for a considerable number of years insufficient voluntary saving will be forthcoming to meet even normal requirements; time will show. In due course the extra war-time savings will, so to speak, be absorbed into the system and the normal tendency to accumulate will be resumed. When this happens the existence of a large dead-weight debt will tend to make them higher in relation to requirements than indicated in the foregoing analysis in each of the cases considered.

It is now time to revert to the problem of a steady advance. We have seen that this may not be achieved save with a steadily rising or falling rate of interest. It is necessary to examine this concept closely.

Any civilized economy is somewhat forward looking; it furnishes itself with equipment; individuals lay by titles. It has some regard to future values. In an advancing community the broad prospect is one of an increase in the value of factors of production in terms of their products. But although an individual may in certain circumstances mortgage his future income, a society cannot collectively anticipate good times; it has to wait for them to accrue.

Physical equipment is a link between the present and future; so are efficient organizations which enjoy the

" know-how " of various forms of production and selling, and are expected to continue using it. The prospective yield of the equipment and of the shares of the firms are reflected in their present prices. Allowance is made for the uncertainties in the situation ; and the rate of interest plays a part. The rate of interest also governs the present value of promises to pay future annuities. These promised annuities may be derived from the anticipated earnings of existing equipments or firms, or they may not. The values of these various titles to revenues have for long been fixed in organized markets.

There is, in the real world, no steady advance. Inventions come irregularly and we have the perplexities of the trade cycle. And the future is necessarily involved in great uncertainty. Therefore we cannot expect the valuations of securities in organized markets to follow a steady course of progress.

None the less we are entitled to consider whether organized markets have any tendency to prognosticate in their valuations continued downward or upward movements of interest. Going deeper, we may ask whether the method of borrowing money at fixed interest for substantial terms of years or without redemption date is compatible with a regular downward or upward movement of interest.

Consider $2\frac{1}{2}$ per cent stock due for redemption at a precise date twenty years hence and suppose this is valued at $95\frac{1}{4}$. In principle this might signify any of an infinite number of opinions about the future course of interest. Of these the simplest is that interest is at present $2\frac{3}{4}$ per cent (approximately) and that upward or downward movements in the interval are equally likely. But it might equally well signify the opinion that interest is now at $3\frac{1}{2}$ per cent and will move downwards steadily to

2 per cent during the intervening 20 years. This would mean that the value of the stock was expected to move on a regular curve, rising substantially in the earlier years and during its course passing through a range of values well above par. It might signify many similar patterns.

Which of these things the present valuation does signify may be ascertained by comparing it with the valuations of stocks with different redemption dates. The assumption that the valuation represents a firm opinion that the interest rate will have a regular movement leads in general to paradoxical results. Thus the assumption of a movement from $3\frac{1}{2}$ to 2 per cent over 20 years would give $2\frac{1}{2}$ per cent stock due for redemption at a precise date 10 years hence a *lower* value (94 approximately) than that due for redemption in 20 years.

The value of stock having no redemption date becomes indeterminate unless we put a term to the fall in the rate of interest. Supposing it were assumed that the fall in interest would be terminated at 2 per cent at the end of 20 years, irredeemable $2\frac{1}{2}$ per cent stock should stand at approximately $112\frac{1}{2}$. Such a quotation alongside those for the $2\frac{1}{2}$ per cent stocks with fixed redemption dates already cited would be a paradox. But if one extrapolated the arithmetical fall in interest for ten years further, namely to $1\frac{1}{4}$ per cent, $2\frac{1}{2}$ per cent consols would stand at no less a figure than 150 (approx.).

These results do not seem to conform with market behaviour as it has been known at any time. In the face of oscillations due to the trade cycle such forward valuations would hardly be possible. Even were the trade cycle eliminated, however, it is difficult to see how the market could deal with stock without redemption date on this basis. Yet this is very important, since ordinary shares issued by good companies themselves constitute claims on a revenue no final term for which is set. Thus it would be natural for the value at which the market would accept an issue of such shares to be related to that of irredeemable gilt-edged stock, standing below it by a margin deemed sufficient to cover the extra risk. And the valuation of such share issues is perhaps the most critical way in which the rate of interest plays its part in stimulating or retarding industrial expansion.

I think that those who have conceived of a steadily falling rate of interest would argue the matter differently. They would hold — at first sight more realistically — that the rate is fixed from time to time under the influence of supply and demand at the moment, each new fall coming, so to speak, as a surprise to the market, and not therefore having been discounted in previous valuations.

Supply consists of aggregated savings including current savings, and demand of all assets including dead-weight debt and assets currently coming into existence or planned. These two totals have a common item, namely past aggregations of savings which are equal to the total of assets and titles already existing, so that the rate of interest is made to vary, on this argument, in response to current decisions to create new assets and current decisions to save out of income, in such wise as to secure equality between these two sets of decisions. But this line of approach is almost as unrealistic as the other.

The existing stock of assets and titles is always large by comparison with new additions. It is not to be supposed that the market will revalue this great stock in response to every chance disequilibrium between the planned increments of demand and supply. It is not to be supposed that it takes no regard for the future, being willing to mark stock up to 200 (in order to absorb current savings) when it is fairly certain that the stock will come down again to 100 in the near future.

It is partly due to the fact that this does not happen that economists have been driven to introduce such concepts as forced saving, involuntary dis-saving, discrepancies between ex-ante and ex-post saving or between ex-ante and ex-post capital outlay, and finally to Keynesian theory, which I propose to consider at the beginning of the next lecture.

It has been in the minds of economists that there is, in the world of ideal concepts, some banking policy, which, if carried out, would prevent forced saving or discrepancies between ex-ante and ex-post capital outlay ever occurring. I suggest, on the contrary, that economic theory has so far advanced no valid propositions regarding how the rate of interest would behave in response to an ideal banking policy designed to maintain a steady advance. Static theory implies that saving is zero and is inappropriate. Dynamic theory strives after the concept of a steadily falling rate of interest, but I do not think that market conditions have been envisaged in which this could become a reality.

FUNDAMENTAL DYNAMIC THEOREMS

At the conclusion of the last lecture I discussed two approaches to the problem of what might govern the market rate of interest in a steadily advancing community. I hasten to add that both these approaches, though at first sight appropriate to the problem in hand and conformable with economic analysis generally, were totally unrealistic.

On the one hand we considered the possibility that the market having looked forward and in its wisdom assessed that fundamental conditions required a falling rate of interest in the coming period, so marked the values of gilt-edged securities of various maturities that, with expectations unchanged, a steady fall in the rate of yield would eventuate between the present and the dates of maturity. It appeared clearly that this was to attribute far too much foresight to the market and that any assessment of this sort implies a valuation of securities of various maturities which is altogether in conflict with the whole mass of our market experience. It is also very difficult to see what, on this basis, the market could do with securities without redemption date.

The other line of approach went to the opposite extreme and supposed that the market in long-dated securities would be governed by the current balance between supply and demand for new capital.[1] Short-

---

[1] It is not implied that the doctrine in this extreme form has been held by recent writers.

sighted though the market may be it is not as short-sighted as all this. An adjustment of the security values to the monthly balance between the supply of and the demand for new capital would surely mean variations of at least the order of 1 or 2 per cent in the rate of interest, *i.e.* of 50 or 100 per cent in the value of irredeemable securities. The idea that the market will, in the course of a short period, mark perfectly good British Government securities, now at 140, now at 70, is quite wide of the mark. Such a procedure would be wrong from every point of view. Especially is this so when one recalls that according to this theory the alleged changes in the market prices of these securities should occur even if there were no change in expectations as regards the future. Changes of expectation may cause big changes in Stock Exchange values, albeit probably not changes big enough to secure the monthly balance in the supply and demand for new capital; but there is no reason whatever to suppose that such changes of expectation will occur, indeed it would be quite fantastic to suppose that they would occur every time there was a need, from the point of view of the monthly balance, to get a big change in prices. I class this method of approach, therefore, as being quite as unrealistic as the other.

The approach by Keynes to the problem of the market rate of long-term interest, whatever criticisms one may bring against it, is much more realistic than either of these. The future is not left out of account, although Keynes did not think that the Stock Exchange took a very long view! Still there is no question in the Keynes analysis of the market fixing present values at levels that are widely different from what they judge the future will have in store. On the other hand no definite curve of future prices is deemed to be foreseen. On the contrary, it is the essence of the theory that the market is very largely uncertain as to what is to happen in the future. In Dynamics we must not, any more than in Statics, think away uncertainty. Even if we postulate that the fundamental conditions are changing steadily, so as to determine, if all could be assessed accurately, a steady rate of advance and therewith a steady fall of interest, we must not postulate that it is known that these conditions will be such.

In Keynes interest is reduced to nothing more than a risk premium against fluctuations about which we are uncertain. Is the rate of interest unduly high, if it is deemed to serve no other function than that of being a risk premium? After all a change of $\frac{1}{2}$ per cent may mean a change of some 20 per cent in capital values, and $2\frac{1}{2}$ per cent is perhaps a not unduly high premium to charge for bearing this risk.

Criticisms have been made of this theory on the ground that it leaves interest suspended, so to speak, in a void, there being interest because there is interest. Professor Robertson's subtle thoughts on economics have for long solaced the hearts of economists, and great weight is due to any criticism he makes. I quote from page 25 of his *Essays in Monetary Theory*:

> Thus the rate of interest is what it is because it is expected to become other than it is; if it is not expected to become other than it is there is nothing left to tell us why it is what it is. The organ which secretes it has been amputated, and yet it somehow still exists — " a grin without a cat ". Mr. Plumptre of Toronto, in an unpublished paper, has aptly compared the position of the lenders of money under this theory with that of an insurance company which charges its clients a premium, the only risk against which it insures them being the risk that its premium will be raised. If we ask what

ultimately governs the judgments of wealth owners as to why the rate of interest should be different in the future from what it is to-day, we are surely led straight back to the fundamental phenomena of productivity and thrift.

Or again, Mr. Hicks writes : " But to say that the rate of interest on perfectly safe securities is determined by nothing else but uncertainty of future interest rates seems to leave interest hanging by its own boot straps; one feels an obstinate conviction that there must be more in it than that ". Mr. Hicks, however, does not base himself upon productivity and thrift but upon the cost incurred by the marginal transferer of money into short-dated securities, long-term interest being on this view ultimately governed by short-term interest.

These criticisms suggest that the Keynes theory of interest is circular; there is interest because the rate of interest is expected to change; in fine, there is interest, because there is expected to be interest. But why is there expected to be interest? And so, why is there interest?

I do not think that this criticism is decisive. Surely there are some phenomena of the mind — and interest is nothing but a phenomenon of the mind, the resultant of thoughts and opinions, hopes and fears, itself only a promise, finally indeed an act, but one solely originating in the will of the two parties, not a physical phenomenon at all — surely there are mental phenomena to which the dictum may correctly be applied that there is nothing true but thinking makes it so.

And I am inclined to think that this account of interest hanging by its own boot straps is an exaggeration. Consider a security with a certain par value due in twenty years, carrying $2\frac{1}{2}$ per cent. Without interest the present value of £100 of such stock would be £150. This is a definite sum of money. But the market does not value the stock at £150, but at some lower figure, say, £100, to allow for the fact that the holder cannot be sure of getting the exact calculated sum, whatever it may be, between £150 and £100 at a date of his own choosing in the next twenty years. But, it will be objected that if there is no interest, and known that there will not in any case be any interest, will he not have a certainty of getting this appropriate sum? But this assumption is too far-reaching. In fairness to Keynes, I do not think we are entitled to assume, in rebutting the theory of liquidity preference, a world in which it was known that there never could be any interest, presumably a world in which there never had been any interest! And are not the critics going a little far? Did Keynes anywhere say that liquidity preference was the sole and only reason why there ever had been or could be interest? Or did he not rather merely say that liquidity preference was the sole determinant of the level of the interest rate?

I am not prepared to reject Keynes's theory, even in the stripped form in which his critics present it, as untenable. It is certainly much more realistic than the other two possible theories I have touched on. On the other hand I do not think that Keynes compels us to suppose that the market in brooding upon future prices, and on the uncertainties thereof, pays no regard whatever to Professor Robertson's productivity and thrift.

And I would add this in defence of Keynes. Some critics imply, perhaps Keynes himself implied, that he was substituting his theory for some well-established orthodox theory, so that, if we reject Keynes, there is something to fall back on. I deny the existence of the alleged orthodox theory, and claim that the Keynes theory ought properly to be regarded as an attempt to fill a void.[1]

[1] I do not imply that his was the first attempt!

If we reject the Keynes theory in whole or in part, we must offer something in its place (as Mr. Hicks does) or acknowledge that we are so far without any theory of interest. It surely cannot be maintained that dealers in the market acting for their own advantage are in a position to evaluate long period trends in the manner described in the last lecture and to mark stocks in such a way as to imply that the yield on them due to interest and appreciation (or depreciation) will move during future years along a curve — if there is a redemption date the curve will often have to rise and fall alternately. Nor is it in the least degree feasible to hold that values are adjusted so as to balance the contemporary increments of demand and supply regardless of the future.

In the case of commodity markets contemporary dis-equilibrium can be made good by absorption into or release from stocks. Now it might at first blush be supposed that jobbers or other dealers by holding stocks and shares on speculative account or taking up bear positions per-form a function precisely analogous to that of dealers in commodity markets. This is an illusion. The operations of dealers in the two kinds of market are similar in that both they tend (or should tend) to iron out fluctuations of prices. But the great difference is that whereas physical commodities can be carried forward through time by storage, it is impossible to do this with " waiting " or " saving " ; it cannot be put into a bottle and transferred from time A to time B. Real assets can, of course, be carried forward through time, pending their use ; com-modity stocks are indeed a particular example of this. But this carry forward is *after* saving has been taken up and embodied in something real. It cannot be carried forward prior to such embodiment.

In the cases both of particular commodities and saving

in general, price oscillation would probably have to be extremely violent to equate output to use day by day. In the former case this oscillation is reduced by the device of storing output for future use. In the case of saving this device is not available and the *modus operandi* of the security markets is different. By preventing these heroic rises in interest changes which might be necessary from time to time to confine investment plans to saving available on that day, they allow those plans to go forward. This progress is achieved, not by the release of stored up " saving " nor as a direct result of the speculators' purchases, but indirectly by reduction of real stocks in some other part of the economy. Conversely when interest rates would be required to fall to zero or below it in order to get a day to day adjustment of the provision of saving to its use, security dealers allow the saving to go forward despite the lack of adequate investment plans, and this is effected through the unwanted accumulation of capital stocks in some other part of the economy.

But the matter does not rest there. To trace its ramifications Keynes brought forward his multiplier theory. What is it that prevents that large oscillation in the value of interest, which would be needed to equate the provision to the use of savings from time to time? According to Keynes, variations in employment and income. What is the orthodox theory in regard to what limits oscillations in the rate of interest? I submit with respect that there is no established traditional theory to be pitted against Keynes's specific theory.

There is a somewhat different line of criticism of Keynes's liquidity preference theory of interest which I confess I have always thought to have substance. Keynes insists that interest is solely the reward for parting with liquidity and not in any sense the reward for waiting.

This insistence has appeared to me to be one-sided and not necessary for his case. It must be agreed, surely he would have to agree, that two activities are necessary before capital can be provided, namely (1) waiting and (2) parting with liquidity. Both activities, anyhow in certain circumstances, have to be rewarded if they are to take place. If a reward for waiting is necessary in order that there shall be waiting, those who want to enjoy the benefit of it will have to pay that reward, the liquidity preference question apart.

A promising line of analysis might seem to be that when there are two activities of this sort both necessary, the user of the end product (viz. capital disposal) will have to pay the price necessary to satisfy the lender in his capacity of waiter or the price necessary to satisfy him in his capacity of parter with liquidity, whichever is higher. There seems to be an assumption in Keynes that the second will be higher, and, in circumstances in which this is so and those only, it is the second that will determine the rate of interest ; in those circumstances and those only the whole of Keynes's argument follows as set out. Keynes would not, I think, have accepted this limitation. He would rest himself on the view that income, the source of saving, is a dependent variable in the whole picture and that the supply schedule of saving will so adjust itself as to conform to the rate of interest established in the market to satisfy liquidity preference whatever that rate might be.

We may grapple with this problem in another way. Accepting the liquidity preference theory of the market rate, there are two possibilities in regard to the relation of this to the supply of saving, only one of which Keynes appears to have considered. And to that extent his *General Theory* may be deemed to lack generality. One case, the case he treated, is where the liquidity preference rate is higher than that rate of interest which would make capital outlay equal to all the saving that would occur at that rate of interest in conditions of full employment. That being so, insufficient capital outlay occurs, and by consequence there is not full employment. But what of the case in which the market rate of interest, as determined by the forces defined by Keynes, established itself at a level at which capital outlay exceeded the volume of saving forthcoming at that rate at full employment? Then we should have an inflationary condition — such as we have now! The present is precisely a situation in which the efforts of the Chancellor of the Exchequer are holding the liquidity preference rate of interest far below the level at which capital outlay would balance saving forthcoming at full employment. Hence the need for controls. If Keynes did not deal with this other case, it may be that at the time of writing he deemed it so far removed from actuality as to have no practical interest. Formally one may say that he has only tackled half his subject.

There is a fundamental difference, however, between the state of affairs as outlined in the Keynesian analysis which arises when the liquidity preference rate is too high and that which — at least in the absence of Keynes to analyse this other half of the field! — we must deem to arise should the liquidity preference rate of interest be too low. In the former case Keynes presents us with what in the absence of fresh disturbing causes can be regarded as a stable equilibrium with involuntary unemployment present. On the other side of the line one would have, it appears, not any kind of equilibrium, but an inflationary condition, an unstable condition of expansion, destined ultimately to be terminated. Capital outlay exceeding

F

saving at full employment, there would be an inflationary pressure with rising prices, an expansion beyond the rate that could be sustained, and in the end some kind of breakdown. Thus we are confronted with asymmetry.

In this connection I should like to remind you of the main difference between Keynes's *Treatise on Money* and his *General Theory*. As you are well aware, he altered his definitions of saving and investment between the two treatises, a matter about which we need not complain too much! In the *Treatise* his concepts of saving and investment, though not identical with, are first cousins to, the concepts of ex-ante saving and investment. In the *Treatise* he envisages two alternative conditions, one in which investment is greater than saving and the other the opposite. The former of these is roughly analogous to the case where the liquidity preference rate of interest is below the level at which capital outlay would be equal to the saving as it then was; capital outlay is thus stimulated. The *General Theory* concentrates attention on the other case. But there is a great difference between the two treatments. In the *Treatise* we get an unstable condition on both sides of the line, viz., progressive expansion on the one side and progressive contraction on the other. In the *General Theory*, on the other hand, Keynes provides for the possibility of a stable equilibrium on the lower side, namely where the liquidity preference rate of interest is above the level required to secure full-employment-capital-outlay. In this, of course, the *General Theory* breaks new ground. It was this to which he attached great importance. It was important. It was in order to get what he thought would be a convenient apparatus for demonstrating this possibility of stable equilibrium on the low side that he abandoned the ex-ante and went over to the ex-post concepts of saving and investment.

I suggest that the *Treatise* may be regarded as his diagnosis of the trade cycle, and the *General Theory* as his diagnosis of chronic unemployment or under production. The *Treatise* does not provide a satisfactory account o. chronic unemployment, because there the conditions in which the liquidity preference rate (to anticipate his later terminology) is too high are essentially conditions of instability, of growing depression. And the opposite conditions are essentially those of gathering momentum. There is no notion of stability at a certain level when the rate of interest is above its proper height, however that may be defined. Thus there is nothing arising from the analysis of the *Treatise* to suggest that in certain circumstances the rate of interest may be chronically too high, that we may have a permanent unemployment problem, over and above that caused by the cycle itself. But the circumstances at the time were such as to suggest that there is in fact a problem of chronic unemployment, needing analysis. The *General Theory* was Keynes's answer. Until that the greater number of economists had lulled themselves with the idea that unemployment, bad as it might be, was a function of frictions, rigidities and the trade cycle. This assumption was first seriously challenged by the *General Theory* and that was itself important. In the light of this it is not perhaps of great moment that Keynes did not in the *General Theory* embark upon an analysis of the other possibility, where the rate as determined by liquidity preference tended chronically to over-stimulate capital outlay.

There is a more important line of criticism on which I wish to dwell briefly. In the *General Theory* the goal of our endeavours, so to speak, is full employment. Management of the rate of interest is to be directed to this goal. But there is another concept, quite different from though not necessarily inconsistent with the idea of full employment, namely a steady rate of progress conformable with fundamental conditions. Of course we wish for a steady rate of progress with full employment, using that expression in not too exaggerated a sense, all along the line. But what of the analysis? Full employment is one thing and a steady rate of progress quite another. To secure full employment in the short period without regard to what may be necessary for securing a steady rate of progress is short-sighted. We shall not have a very sound policy if we envisage treating the problem of unemployment *ad hoc* from month to month without regard to what sustained level of capital outlay is necessary for an advance of the economy in line with what fundamental conditions allow. I am not suggesting that there is anything radically wrong with the Keynesian remedies, but only that they must ultimately be based upon a somewhat different analytical approach and judged by a different criterion.

An interesting point may be noted in passing. If we start from a condition of severe unemployment, some pump-priming — I will not bother about the precise form, but for the moment we may think of that old-fashioned remedy of public works — may be necessary. If we have success, and conditions improve, at some point the acceleration principle must surely come into play, I will not say with precisely what force. As we move forward to full employment capital outlay may well exceed, almost must exceed, the normal level appropriate to the fundamental conditions of our steadily advancing economy. For in this upward phase we are advancing much more rapidly than at the normal steady rate. Therefore if we carry our policy through and approach full employment, there must be a falling off of the capital outlay associated with the abnormal rate of advance, an abnormal rate which may proceed over a year or two. Thus, still speaking in terms of this old-fashioned remedy of public works, the point at which it will be above all necessary to have a large volume of public works to turn on, perhaps a larger volume than in the original pump-priming phase, is when we approach full employment.

Having criticized Keynes for his lack of a dynamic principle, we must return to the consideration of that principle. In our earlier lecture we reached the conclusion that fundamental conditions might require a steadily falling rate of interest. We found great difficulties in envisaging how the capital market could ever succeed in providing such a steady decline.

Static theory does two things. It defines the positions of rate of output and price at which everyone will be willing to carry on. Each person, if you like, is on the most favoured indifference curve which he can reach, and no one sees any means of self-improvement in the circumstances prevailing. Secondly, it has something to say as to how these positions are reached. In this uncertain world we have to proceed by trial and error. A producer tries producing so much. Experience and observation may then suggest that he could enlarge his profit by producing more. If a man is not doing the best for himself the pricing mechanism gives him guidance; it beckons him on or shows him the red light. It does so anyhow in cases in which the preferred position is a stable equilibrium. Of course we know from static theory that there may be more than one position of stable equilibrium, of which one may be better than the other, but will not necessarily be reached if the agent happens to have got into the other; we know that there may be ranges of indeterminacy. These matters are being ever more intensively examined. In a very broad sense, however, we believe that on the assumptions required for static analysis there is a tendency for the various members of the economy to work towards and stay in the best available positions. If demand exceeds supply, the price will rise, and so forth.

The most difficult problem in the static analysis is probably the general level of output — Keynes's problem in fact. Relative levels of the output of each article are well catered for, subject to the secondary difficulties already mentioned. For the general level of output we have had to rely on the balancing of the marginal utility of income with the marginal disutility of work. It is rightly felt to be disturbing to the structure of this theory if long continued "involuntary" unemployment is possible.

The decision by an entrepreneur to increase output has a twofold effect: it alters his relative position and it alters the general level of output. If he is but one unit in a large economy the second-mentioned effect may be unimportant. But may it entail some tendency to set up a cumulative process of expansion? A harvest variation, because widespread, may have more important effects in that direction than changes by an individual.

I will not pause, however, to consider possibilities within the static conditions, but proceed directly to dynamic assumptions. Growth is the aggregated effect of a great number of individual decisions. In the foregoing treatment I have attempted to analyse the main elements in growth, and to indicate the nature of possible lines of advance. This corresponds to the representation of what the positions would be in the equilibrium of a stationary state. But what of the analysis of the stability of that equilibrium? If the rate of growth entailed by the aggregated individual decisions based on trial and error is different from the rate of growth required by the fundamental conditions, are there forces tending to correct that rate and bring it into line with the growth required by the fundamental conditions?

It will not be possible in what follows to keep our minds altogether free of the trade cycle problem. I am afraid that a proper understanding of the relation between the requirements of a steady advance and what the market can provide is very much mixed up with the trade cycle problem. But there are various aspects of that problem, which I propose to leave entirely on one side, particularly those connected with lags. I wish to concentrate attention on one or two aspects that seem to me very closely related to the general dynamic problem.

I propose, if you will allow me, to seek to push forward by reverting to a method of analysis suggested in an article which I wrote in the *Economic Journal* of March 1939, in particular to the fundamental equation there set out. Pending any damaging criticism of that equation, I feel that it is a powerful tool for sorting out the factors involved and would therefore ask you to give attention to it. I shall slightly, but only slightly, alter the notation.

This fundamental equation has two forms. In one it is a truism, in the other a statement of the rate of growth which will leave the various parties satisfied. Neither is directly related to the growth made possible by continuing changes in fundamental conditions. First we may look at the truism. For this purpose I write the equation as follows :

$$GC = s.$$

G, which stands for growth, is the increment of total production in any unit period expressed as a fraction of total production. Thus if the line of steady advance meant an increase in output of 2 per cent per annum, G would be 1/50; or if the unit period chosen was a month, G would be 1/600.

C (capital) is the increase in the volume of goods of all kinds outstanding at the end over that outstanding at the beginning of the period divided by the increment of production in that same period. This seems a somewhat complicated concept, but I hope that you will feel, as the argument proceeds, that it is really a very simple one.

The value of GC is independent of the unit period chosen. Consider one standard unit period and another unit period n times the length of the standard unit. The numerator of G measured for the second-named unit period is n^2 times that of the standard unit period, while the denominator is n times that of the standard unit period (*e.g.* income per annum is twelve times income per month); therefore the value of G measured for the second-mentioned unit period is n times its value mentioned for the standard unit period. The numerator of C for the second-mentioned unit period is n times its numerator measured for the standard unit period, while the denominator of the former is n^2 times the denominator of the latter. Thus the value of C for the second-mentioned period is $1/n$ times that of the latter. Thus the value of GC is independent of the unit period chosen.

s is the fraction of income saved. It is not necessary for the following argument to assume that s is constant as G changes. The long analysis in the last lecture did not, I think, yield a more convenient way of expressing the value of saving likely to be volunteered than as a fraction of income. On the whole that seemed to be the most probable value for the saving required if an advance was to be steady at constant interest. It was recognized, however, that in crucial cases saving as a fraction of income might not be constant.

All that is required for the argument immediately to follow is that any changes in s, *i.e.* saving expressed as a fraction of income, should be small by comparison with experimental changes in G. And this requirement is clearly fulfilled. Without any great revolution G might easily change from 2 to 6 per cent. This clearly could not cause saving to be trebled. The extreme case of saving being as low as 2 per cent of income and all extra income, due to a rise of G, being saved may be ruled out. If saving is greater than 2 per cent then for saving as a fraction of income to increase by as much as G, consumption would have to be cut (in all probable circumstances by large amounts) as income rose, and this, too, may be ruled out.

To meet the criticism that this equation gives too much emphasis to the acceleration principle, we may insert a term which may be interpreted as liberally as you wish. Let us write the equation

$$GC = s - k,$$

where k consists of current additions to capital (the value thereof to be expressed as a fraction of current income) the worth-whileness of which is not deemed to have any immediate relation to current requirements. k is in fact the capital outlay of a long-range character, capital outlay which no one expects to see justified or not justified within a fairly short period. In the long run k must disappear, for in the long run all capital outlay is justified by the use to which it is put. But it may be very important to separate it out in the short period. In the short period make k as large as you please. Units of equipment, etc., which are included in k must be omitted in the computation of C. If k is very large (as in war) and exceeds s,

C may become negative, and we shall then have an inflationary situation.

C is the addition to capital, but need not consist exclusively or even mostly of capital goods. It is merely the accretion during the period of all goods (less those goods which are included in k). This equation does not make any explicit reference to goods in process. The varying level of these is no doubt important, but I deliberately do not distinguish them because I believe that we are on the way to certain basic truths, which are independent of complications that have to be introduced when we seek to build up a more detailed picture of the whole process. I emphasize that this equation is necessarily true. It follows from the definitions of the terms.[1] It is a dynamic equation since it contains G, which refers to the rate of increase. I also commend to you its extreme simplicity. I should like to think that it might serve as a target for frequent attack, like Fisher's famous truism $MV = PT$. I will only say this. Do not seek to criticize it by reference to alternative equations or formulae which do not contain a dynamic term such as G. That would not be playing the game. I feel that I shall have achieved something really important if in the discussion and criticism of this formula I can habituate the critics to thinking in dynamic terms. I know of no alternative formulation, in the world of modern economic theory, of any dynamic principle of comparable generality. We must start with some generality however imperfect. We shall never go ahead if we remain in a world of trivialities

---

[1] It can easily be seen, by the cancellation of common terms, that it is reducible to the truism that ex-post " investment " is equal to ex-post saving.

Let Y stand for income, I for investment and S for saving.

$$GC = \frac{\Delta Y}{Y} \cdot \frac{I}{\Delta Y} \text{ and } s = \frac{S}{Y}.$$

or fine points. It is useless to refine and refine when there are no basic ideas present at all.

We now come to the form of the equation which expresses the equilibrium of a steady advance. I write this:

$$G_w C_r = s.$$

Repeating the terminology of my earlier article I call G_w the warranted rate of growth. This has nothing whatever to do with the rate of growth determined by the fundamental conditions of population increase, etc., which was discussed earlier. This equation expresses the condition in which producers will be content with what they are doing.

How are we to compare the equilibrium of a steady advance with a static equilibrium? In the static equilibrium producers remain content with their existent rate of output. They look upon their work and they see that it is good. On a broad definition this need not preclude variations in particular commodities. We may suppose that some producers find that the demand is falling off and others that it is increasing, in fact that not all individuals are content to rest in their present condition, but are subject to forces requiring them to adjust upwards or downwards. But if the fundamental conditions as a whole are stationary, the amount of contraction suggested by this condition of markets for various specialities should be equal to the amount of expansion suggested by other markets. An adjustment is made, and the static equilibrium equations prescribe the new values at which the various kinds of output will eventually settle down after a shorter or longer period.

The same circumstances apply to a steady advance. This concept need not preclude the more rapid advance in certain sectors, lower advances or even declines in others. In this case, however, there will be an over-all tendency to advance somewhat, namely, if the short period conditions are right for a steady advance, at the rate G_w. The decision by each entrepreneur to continue producing at the rate he has produced or to produce something more is no doubt determined both by the satisfactory or unsatisfactory character of the results of his previous decisions as experienced to date — a point upon which the lag analysis lays primary stress — and also by a reasonable prognostication of what is to come based on a survey of the particular markets. I define G_w as that over-all rate of advance which, if executed, will leave entrepreneurs in a state of mind in which they are prepared to carry on a similar advance. Some may be dissatisfied and have to adjust upwards or downwards, but the ups and downs should balance out and, in the aggregate, progress in the current period should be equal to progress in the last preceding period.

The equation before us sets out to define the rate of advance which will give satisfaction and lead to its own perpetuation.

C_r is the term for capital requirements. Whereas in the truistic equation there was an ex-post term expressing the amount of capital goods actually produced per period, C_r is an equilibrium term expressing requirements for new capital. C_r is defined analogously with C, namely as the requirement for new capital divided by the increment of output to sustain which the new capital is required. C_r is thus the required capital coefficient.

This definition is based on the idea that existing output can be sustained by existing capital and that additional capital is only required to sustain additional output. This follows from the assumption that the capital/income ratio is constant, *i.e.* that the length of the production process is unchanged and this follows from the two assumptions on which we are at present working, namely, (1) that inventions are neutral and (2) that the rate of interest is constant. The equation must be modified in a way that I shall presently describe when we have to deal with the case of the production processes getting more roundabout.

Of course this does not imply that all inventions are neutral. There is no need to make such a rigid requirement, which would of course be altogether unrealistic. In the case of certain goods an invention may come forward greatly raising the amount of capital required for the more efficient production of a given quantum of goods. In other cases the " invention " may take the form of an improvement in managerial methods — the point in which some say we are much further behind the Americans than in our physical capital equipment — whereby a given plant is made to yield a higher output of goods. What we are postulating in our dynamic approach to these problems is that on average all the various inventions and improvements accruing in a unit period are neutral, those requiring more capital per unit of output balancing the effect of those which require less. On this assumption the existing capital of the country, always of course changing its precise form in all the different sectors, can sustain the existing output. New capital is required in relation to new output (whether the new output is due to an increase of population or an increase of output per head). C_r is of course a marginal notion; it is the new capital required to sustain the output which will satisfy the demands for consumption arising out of consumers' marginal addition to income.[1] Thus

---

[1] After a recession, when there is much redundant capacity, C_r is temporarily reduced to a low level.

C_r, the marginal requirement for new capital, may not be equal to the capital coefficient in the economy as a whole. But as a condition for a steady advance we have to assume that C_r does not change over the range of income increase that occurs during the postulated period of steady advance. You may think that all these assumptions involved in the definition of C_r taken together are rather large, but I suggest that they define the simplest possible case from which we can well proceed to develop various complications.

It may suggest itself to your minds that the frequent occurrence of inventions or frequent changes of taste would lead to demands for fresh saving even although both kinds of change were on balance of neutral character. Will not new installations be required in consequence of the changes, and new savings, in order to finance them? In general this does not appear to be the case. Provided that the tempo of change is recognized by entrepeneurs, they will fix their depreciation allowances accordingly. These will be higher in a progressive than in a stagnant economy. In particular cases, however, unforeseen changes might be so great as to throw whole firms into liquidation before they had had time to write down the obsolete sector of their assets to zero, and it could be argued that this loss of real capital will not be offset by the longevity, in other firms, of assets which last beyond expectation, since assets cannot be written down below zero. Strictly, losses such as these should be deducted from positive savings in fixing the value of s. Alternatively new installations of a value equal to the loss of incompletely written off assets in the hands of bankrupt firms might be included in k. The existence of such losses does not affect the argument which follows.

I now ask you to look closely at the two equations set

84

out. The former, you remember, is a truistic equation which must be satisfied whatever advance or recession takes place. The latter expresses the fact that if the advance is to be maintained, C, the quantity of the addition to capital actually accruing, must be what is needed. This capital, as I have already pointed out, covers both equipment and stock-in-trade. I am not at present basing myself upon the distinction between durable and non-durable goods or upon that between producer and consumer goods. C consists in part of consumer goods, including non-durable consumer goods. In an advancing community goods in the pipe-line, shops, warehouses, transit, and producers' stores, have to increase in proportion to turnover. All these goods are part of capital. The rise or fall of goods in the pipe-line above or below the required level may be just as big a factor as the margins of unwanted equipment or shortage of equipment in depressing or stimulating the system.

Taking these two equations together, we can see a relation of the utmost simplicity, and I ask you to join with me in thinking it extraordinarily impressive. The greater G, the lower C. That can hardly be questioned. Consequently if G has a value above G_w, C will have a value below C_r. I see no way of escape from that. If C has a value below C_r, this means that on balance producers and traders find the goods in the pipe-line or the equipment insufficient to sustain existing turnover. Let me repeat : if the value G is above that of G_w, the value of C must be below that of C_r ; there will be insufficient goods in the pipe-line and/or insufficient equipment, and orders will be increased. If the value G is above the value G_w, that is if the actual growth is above the line of growth consistent with a steady advance, orders will be increased. And, of course, conversely. This strikes me as an extraordinarily simple and notable demonstration of the instability of an advancing system. Around the line of advance, which, if adhered to, would alone give satisfaction, centrifugal forces are at work, causing the system to depart further and urther from the required line of advance.

G is a quantity determined from time to time by trial and error, by the collective trials and errors of vast numbers of people. It would be great luck if their collective appraisals caused them to hit precisely upon the value G_w. But if they do not do so their experience will tend to drive them farther and farther from it. This kind of instability has nothing to do with the effect of lags, and strikes me as more fundamental. The only way in which this conclusion could be upset would be by the suggestion that variations in G would cause equally large variations in the value of s. But this is clearly unacceptable for reasons already stated. It is not thinkable, for instance, that saving as a fraction of income could be multiplied by 4 in consequence of a change in the increase of income from 1 per cent to 4 per cent. The only case in which anything of this sort could possibly happen would be if the value of k was almost as great as that of s, that is in which almost all savings were absorbed in capital outlay which had no relation to the requirements of current demand.

So far then we have two propositions. (i) There is a line of advance which, if adhered to, would leave producers content with what they had done. A small point that will readily occur to you is that perhaps C_r should be deemed to have a value slightly lower than the required amount of capital, lower, that is, by the amount necessary to keep producers moving forward on the line of advance. If C_r were precisely equal to requirements they might lapse into a stationary condition.

86

(ii) If the aggregated result of trial and error by numerous producers gives a value for G which is different from G_w, there will not be any tendency to adapt production towards G_w, but, on the contrary, a tendency to adapt production still farther away from it, whether on the higher or lower side.

Next it is desirable to relate these two equations to that steady rate of advance determined by fundamental conditions, which has been so much discussed already. We may set this out in the form of an equation as follows:

$$G_n C_r = \text{or} \neq s.$$

G_n ($_n$ for natural) is the rate of advance which the increase of population and technological improvements allow. It has no direct relation to G_w.

G_n represents the line of output at each point on which producers of all kinds will be satisfied that they are making a correct balance between work and leisure; it excludes the possibility of " involuntary " unemployment. G_w is the entrepreneurial equilibrium; it is the line of advance, which, if achieved, will satisfy profit takers that they have done the right thing; in Keynesian fashion it contemplates the possibility of growing " involuntary " unemployment. Thus the plot thickens. We have not only to consider divergences of G and G_w but also those of G_w from G_n.

In the first place it is to be observed that G_n sets a limit to the maximum average value of G over a long period. After a recession G may attain a higher value than G_n for a considerable period. But it is not possible to maintain growth at a greater rate for an indefinite period than the increase of population and technological improvements (both being expressed in G_n) allows.

Secondly, the relation of G_n to G_w is clearly of crucial importance in determining whether the economy over a term of years is likely to be preponderatingly lively or depressed. A paradox is involved. Whenever G exceeds G_w there will be a tendency for a boom to develop; and conversely. Now if G_n exceeds G_w there is no reason why G should not exceed G_w for most of the time. Consequently there is no reason why the economy should not enjoy a recurrent tendency to develop boom conditions. But if G_w exceeds G_n, then G must lie below G_w for most of the time, since the average value of G over a period cannot exceed that of G_n. Therefore in such circumstances we must expect the economy to be prevailingly depressed. This is paradoxical, since, at first blush, one would suppose it to be a good thing that the line of entrepreneurial contentment should be one implying an attempt to push forward always at a greater rate than fundamental conditions allow. Would not this make for a constantly buoyant economy, a tendency always towards full employment? Analysis reveals the opposite to be the case. It is the departures from G_w not the value of G_w itself which have paramount influence in producing boom and slump. If the value of G_w is too great (greater than that of G_n) there will be a prevailing tendency for departures to be in a downward direction. From that there is no escape. I believe that this paradox is very near the heart of the contrast between Keynesian economics and classical economics. Saving *is* a virtue and beneficial so long as G_w is below G_n. While it is disastrous to have G_w above G_n, it is not good to have it too far below, for in that case, although we may have plenty of booms and a frequent tendency to approach full employment, the high employment will be of an inflationary and thereby unhealthy character. In these circumstances saving is a virtue since, by raising G_w, it enables us to have good employment without inflation. But if G_w is above G_n saving is a force making for depression.

It is far from my purpose to give a finished theory of the trade cycle. Lags, psychological, monetary and other factors, no doubt play their part. I should suggest that no theory can be complete which neglects the fundamental causes of instability expressed in the equations which have been set out.

The following points are, however, tentatively advanced.

1. In a revival, in which unemployed resources are brought back to work, G stands above G_n. When full employment is reached it must be reduced to G_n. If G_n stands below G_w then a slump is inevitable at that point, since G has to fall below G_w and will, for the time being, be driven progressively downwards.

2. G_w itself fluctuates in the trade cycle. Even if saving as a fraction of income is fairly steady in the long run, it is not likely to be so in the short run. There is some tendency for saving in the short period to be a residual between earnings and normal habits of consumption. Companies are likely to save a large fraction of short period increases of net receipts. Thus even if G_w is normally below G_n it may rise above it in the later stages of an advance, and, if it does so, a vicious spiral of·depression is inevitable when full employment is reached. If G_w has not been raised above G_n during the course of the advance and there is continued pressure to expand when full employment is reached, then the consequent inflation of prices and profit will sooner or later raise G_w above G_n and thus precipitate the vicious spiral of depression.

3. Before full employment is reached G may have to be reduced owing to the increasing difficulty of transferring labour and other resources to their required uses

as employment gets better. If G_w is substantially above G_n, the G curve may intersect the G_w curve some time before full employment is reached, thus making a vicious spiral of depression inevitable at this point.

4. If G_w is very substantially above G_n, G may never rise very far above G_w during the revival owing to mobility difficulties, and in this case maintenance of the revival may be precarious, and a vicious spiral of depression may be precipitated long before full employment is reached.

While the equations clearly show the instability of an advancing economy, they do not in themselves provide very good tools for analysing the course of the slump. It is probably necessary for that purpose to draw a distinction between durable and non-durable capital. It should be noticed that C is positive if the quantity of capital is moving in the same direction as the level of income. In a slump what matters is that circulating capital should be reduced. The existence of surplus fixed equipment in those trades whose output is shrinking — the output of some may continue to expand under longer period influences in a slump — is not in itself a force making for a further downward adjustment, since orders cannot be reduced below zero. On the other hand a pipe line filled fuller than appropriate to a falling turnover will cause a further contraction of orders.

Consequently in a slump the value of C_r will be lower than usual, being confined to the requirements for circulating capital. Thus the negative value to which $s - k$ has to fall in order to check a certain rate of recession is not nearly so great as the positive value to which it has to rise in order to check the same rate of upward movement.

It is well known that in trade-cycle study gross capital outlay and gross saving are more serviceable concepts than net outlay and saving. During a decline gross outlay on durable plant over part of the field may be nil. A sort of equilibrium of decline would thus be reached in which the negative value of s (gross) minus k minus such capital (considered as a fraction of income) as was required for that part of industry which were still expanding despite the slump, was equal to the rate of decline multiplied by a much reduced capital coefficient consisting of the amount of circulating capital that could be dispensed with in consequence of the decline.

Gross capital requirements, however, do not, like net requirements, depend primarily on the rate of increase of output, but to some extent also on the total level of output. In the early part of the slump these may be reduced to nil (in the contracting sectors), because the old machines or other fixed equipments need not be replaced at the end of their working life owing to reduced output. But sooner or later the requirements for replacements must become positive, if any output at all is to be maintained. The consequent reduction in C_r (a rise in the numerical value of its numerator reduces its algebraic value) may reduce it below C. The actual reduction of capital stock becomes greater than what is convenient. This will arrest the downward movement and turn it into an upward one.

This account of the complete cycle makes no claim to be fully satisfactory. It requires supplementing by the findings of other methods of approach to cycle study.

Thus there are two distinct sets of problems both for analysis and policy, namely: (1) the divergence of G_w from G_n; and (2) the tendency of G to run away from G_w. The former is the problem of chronic unemployment, the latter the trade cycle problem.

First as regards analysis. According to classical doctrine, if there is general unemployment owing to any cause, wages will tend to fall; if wages are none the less maintained in these circumstances, continuance of un-employment is thereby rendered inevitable. This is tantamount to saying that a reduction of wages would be a cure for the unemployment.

You are all familiar with Keynes's views about the effect of wage reduction. I may remind you in passing that his theory and the practical recipes that flow from it relate to a closed system, that being the problem on which he was concentrating his mind. Now that the problem of our foreign trade has become such a predominant one, we have to temper Keynesian policy by reference to it. Keynes's diagnosis may have introduced some measure of levity about the harm that might be done by money wage increases not warranted by the situation.

Of course under the Bretton Woods regime unjustified increases in money wages may be offset by reductions in the foreign exchange rates. None the less they will not be helpful. The working of the International Monetary Fund will in any case bristle with problems, and it is most undesirable that Britain, one of its main pillars, should add to its problems by frequent requests that the value of sterling be reduced. Nor, I think, is the progressive deterioration of the goods value of a currency desirable on other grounds. We do not want savings to go down the drain, especially at this time when they have become more widely diffused and when we hope that the savings of all citizens will grow progressively.

The wage-reduction remedy should be considered under the two heads set out. First as regards the excess of G_w over G_n. It must be remembered that in this investigation of trends, a once-over reduction has no meaning. Does the situation require a year-by-year reduction? This would have no direct effect on G_n.

Would it tend to depress G_w? There is no reason to suppose that it would. Unless output per head is actually falling through time, it does not seem natural to suppose that a steady reduction of money wages is required. On the contrary it seems that a steady reduction of money wages would inflame the difficulties. An upward tendency in the goods value of money certainly increases corporate saving for the reasons stated in the first lecture, and probably increases surplus corporate saving. A steady reduction in money wages would entail an upward movement in the goods value of money. The effect of the reduction would therefore be to raise G_w and so take it still further away from G_n. Thus the chronic tendency to depression would be intensified. We conclude that in an economy tending predominantly to depression a steady reduction of money wages would be injurious.

How does this alleged remedy stand in relation to the trade cycle problem of a run-away of G from G_w? There are two questions: (1) Would a once-over wage reduction give a fillip to output? (2) Would output be sustained at a higher level in consequence of the fillip?

The answer to the second question depends on the nature and causes of the recession. If before the set-back an advance had been proceeding at a rate not too much in excess of G_n and with perhaps some slack of resources still to be taken up, and the set-back was due to some particular adverse event which had sent the system into a downward spin, then a fillip — due to a wage reduction or any other cause — might be useful. It might serve to restore the system to where it was before and thus enable it to proceed on a healthy line of advance. Even if the fillip had in itself no tendency to raise the marginal efficiency of capital nor reduce the propensity to save, it might be of benefit to employment, since on this hypothesis the marginal efficiency of capital before the set-back was sufficient to maintain employment, the present low marginal efficiency being merely due to the decline in activity consequent on the set-back.

But if before the set-back G and G_w were both considerably in excess of G_n and the system approaching full employment, a mere fillip will be in vain. If the system is jerked up to a higher level of employment, it will merely relapse again. If the trouble is an excessive G_w, the wage reduction can do no good even if it does give a fillip. I am of the opinion that an analysis of the effects of a wage reduction which does not use the growth factor as a tool can throw no light on such a situation.

Would a wage reduction have any tendency to give a fillip (in a closed system)? It is important to stress that the fillip, if any, which it might give would be due entirely to the increased consumption by rentiers. In a closed economy in which income could be exhaustively classified as wages (including salaries and fees of all kinds) and profits, a reduction of wages would entail a fully proportional reduction of prices and profits.[1] This would be so unless the profit-taking class accompanied their wage reductions by an increase of personal consumption. In practice, having tender consciences, they would be more likely to do the opposite. Since the economy would receive an equal fillip by an increase of profit-takers' consumption, without any wage reduction, the fillip in question should not be attributed to the wage reduction. The rentiers, on the other hand, will receive a higher goods income in consequence of the fall of money wages and prices and it would be natural for them to increase their consumption; to the extent that they do so the

[1] For a proof of this proposition, see *Economic Journal*, March, 1934, page 23.

goods income of profit takers will also be enlarged. Thus the fillip given by wage reduction consists in essence of the provision of more purchasing power to the rentiers. In so far as they are an important element, this may be of substantial importance. The effectiveness of the fillip depends on the causes of the recession, as already explained.[1]

Whether it is desirable to list such a remedy as a standing order to be applied from time to time, even if it were practical to do so, is doubtful. While I have already urged that we should not wish to destroy the purchasing power of past savers by monetary inflation, it is another matter to raise that purchasing power artificially from time to time. An enlargement of the purchasing power of rentiers at the expense of other sharers in the national dividend is not warranted in equity and tends to reduce the incentive to the more active elements in the community, whether the enlarged payments in terms of goods have to be charged onto the receipts of industry or predominantly, as when the national debt is very large, onto the taxpayers.

We must now turn to the question of interest rates. That a reduction of these would tend to produce the desired effect is agreed, although there may be doubt whether the weapon would be potent enough to cause revival in all circumstances. Where there is disagreement is whether in circumstances of falling employment there is any natural tendency for the rates of interest to move down, for instance under the pressure of an excess of loanable funds, to the level required to restore employment.

[1] It is also possible, of course, that the wage reduction might give a fillip by inducing entrepreneurs to increase capital outlay, whether there was any observed increase in consumption or not. It seems more probable that they would wait for some tangible profit to accrue before embarking on this course.

It must be remembered that there are two problems, the divergence of G_w from G_n and the runaway of G from G_w. If G_w implies a steeper gradient than G_n what will be the position of the rate of interest? Certainly a progressive fall in the rate of interest is the appropriate remedy, vouchsafed by classical and Keynesian economics alike.

Hitherto we have been working on the assumption that inventions have been neutral. To meet the case of their not being so, we may introduce another term into the equilibrium equation. Let d (for deepening) stand for the value of new capital installations during the unit period, expressed for convenience as a fraction of income, involved in the lengthening of the production process. If inventions are " capital saving ", d is negative. Thus,

$$G_w C_r = s - d.$$

It may seem artificial to separate d from C_r. But it is logically possible; and it is right in principle. We want to keep C_r segregated as that capital requirement which essentially belongs to the growth of output as such, from the requirement for increased capital per unit of output.

d may have a positive value because of the nature of the inventions occurring. It may also have a positive value because the rate of interest is falling. Our aim should be to get such a progressive reduction in the rate of interest that

$$G_w C_r = s - d = G_n C_r.$$

If d is positive, C_r will increase through time, and may eventually become so great as to enable us to dispense with d. At that point interest need fall no further. A positive value for d incidentally serves to raise G_n. A falling rate of interest may also — and this is of course important if it so turns out — reduce s.

The question we now have to ask is whether there will be any natural tendency for the rate of interest to come down sufficiently. This is the crux of the matter, the crux, perhaps, of that modern economic situation to which we shall revert, when the post-war shortages cease. This is where the lack of adequate dynamic theory is particularly unfortunate. That theory tells us that a falling rate of interest is necessary if the economy is to advance at its potential rate and reasonably full employment is to be maintained. But whereas static theory not only defines a position of equilibrium but indicates how, through the laws of supply and demand, the economy tends to move into that position, dynamic theory has not so far shown how or whether the market, as subject to the forces that normally operate upon it, will tend to mark the rate of interest down at an appropriate pace.

Keynes's theory, with all its imperfections upon it, does definitely point to a negative answer. Even if the market could form a fairly clear view as to the future trend — which it cannot, since inventions which may be capital requiring, are in essence unpredictable — none the less the lack of certainty would make it demand a risk premium (measuring liquidity preference) for long-term loans. Thus the present rate would be somewhat above the level appropriate to the present situation and to the changing level most likely to be required in future ; and, as each future period will in due course become a present one, this liquidity factor which affects the present rate will also affect future rates to an unknown extent and so prevent the right levels of future rates being made the basis of an argument now. And so we get back again to a rate of interest which is hanging by its own boot-straps. How escape from this ?

The long-term problem is also complicated by the

short-term problem. Getting G_w into equality with G_n over the long period would not by itself present a run-away of G downwards from G_n from time to time. Changes in the market rate due to natural forces clearly will not prevent this; and I shall argue in the next lecture that no Bank Rate policy, however heroic, would be likely to prevent it. (It does not follow that we need despair of an effective contra-cyclical policy.) During the periods in which G is low and unemployment high, clearly less saving will accrue than would otherwise. The loss of savings, which in the aggregate will be large, must affect the long-run course of the interest rate. Thus it would be relevant for an all-wise market to ask how great and how prolonged the downward run-aways of G in future are likely to be. But it will not get an answer.

Critics of Keynes, disliking the divorce which his theory seems to entail between the forces affecting the rate of interest and the supply and demand for savings, have urged that we must consider the stream of loanable funds coming into the market and their tendency to depress the rate of interest as activity falls off. They have to call time-lags to their aid. Strictly in Keynesian theory the effect of the multiplier on activity is instantaneous. But there is no doubt an interval in which there is a discrepancy between ex-ante and ex-post investment. If those involved in unintended investment — accumulation of stocks — do not come into the capital market for the loan of funds — they may have had a cash balance at the expense of which they can hold the unwanted stocks — there may be an excess of the supply of funds over the demand. Or again income may continue to be distributed after output has fallen — presumably also at the expense of the cash of firms — and individuals may supply funds to the market accordingly, or may reckon what they will save on the basis of their income in the last preceding period instead of the present. I am most reluctant to enter this field of thought. Let it be that at the onset of recession there is a greater presentation of funds in the capital market than the strict doctrine of the multiplier would suggest and a consequent downward movement in the rate of interest.

It is not usually sufficient to prevent the onward movement of the recession. So what does it matter? In due course the multiplier will have its full effect in reducing income and savings. At the end of a depression aggregated savings will be less than they would otherwise have been. The rate of interest as governed by the supply of and demand for savings will be higher than if a steady advance had been maintained. Natural forces will not have served to secure that fall in the rate of interest necessary to absorb all savings accruing through time with the community advancing steadily at reasonably full employment.

I am bound to conclude negatively. It does not appear to be shown that the system will of its own secure a sufficient fall in the rate of interest. There is general agreement that this is the true remedy for unemployment. Unemployment has persisted for years and not been remedied. There is therefore a *prima facie* case for a planned reduction in the rate of interest.

Keynes proposed an assault on it by the methods now being used by the Chancellor of the Exchequer, namely by increasing the amount of liquidity available. This has not proved altogether unsuccessful. It is an unfortunate irony that we should have had a spurt in the policy, no doubt justified by the National Debt position and long-run considerations, just at a time when the short-period situation considered in itself would require an exceedingly high rate of interest.

99

Of course there may be limits to the success of this policy, limits which may appear even before, from a long-range point of view, $G_w C_r$ is reduced to the required level. Ultimately the market may refuse to believe that the rate of interest ought to be any lower, and may absorb an unlimited amount of liquidity rather than mark security prices up further. I shall have to return to this.

It may also be that this assault method will not achieve a steady rate of fall but only a series of bumps. That, however, is not fatal, because there will in any case also be a trade cycle problem requiring separate treatment. This is due to the fact that, quite apart from any failure to get the rate of interest down at the required steady rate, there are bound to be exogenous shocks tending to make G diverge from G_w and setting the trade cycle processes going. There will, for instance, be times in which inventions are not neutral. And there will be other shocks.

For this reason, quite apart from our long-range policy of acting upon the rate of interest, we shall have to have a separate contra-cyclical policy. But of this more hereafter.

(a) THE FOREIGN BALANCE

IT is now necessary to open the doors and consider our economy as having trading relations with a wider economy.

With the development of Keynesian doctrine and especially when this reached the culmination of the *General Theory*, it became plain that some reconsideration of balance-of-trade doctrine would be necessary. I think it is fair to say that the classical theory of the balance of trade did imply full employment. In departmental discussions of this subject, as time went on, much was said about the possibility of unemployment being caused by a monetary restriction, necessitated by the foreign trading position. There was something of the same sort of cleavage between basic principle and what one was allowed to say departmentally as there was, before Wicksell, between the basic doctrine of interest as the reward for saving and what one was allowed to say departmentally about fluctuations in the market rate of interest. When it fell to me to produce a revised edition (which appeared in 1939) of my handbook on *International Economics*, I resolved to endeavour to grapple manfully with this problem; I think I succeeded in producing something which gave a systematic account of the relation between the Keynesian theory of unemployment and balance-of-trade theory. I showed the results to Keynes, as being an attempt to fill an important gap which he had left, but he did not give it his imprimatur. He felt that he would need some time to consider it. On the other hand he raised no fundamental objections to it.

His treatment of the balance of trade in the *Treatise on Money* was manifestly makeshift. He was clearly concentrating his mind upon the problems of a closed system, but felt impelled to say something on the foreign trade question. Consequently he was content to treat a positive balance as a form of " Investment ", and this form of investment was reckoned in along with investment at home to constitute that total investment which he used in his celebrated equation. The *General Theory* did not take the external problem much further, although the development of his theory regarding the internal economy certainly required a similar development on the external side.

My treatment of the balance of trade question went on different lines. It seemed clear to me that the volume of achieved exports bore precisely the same relation to the propensity to import that the volume of capital outlay at home bore to the propensity to save. The right solution of the problem therefore seemed to be to conflate the propensity to save and the propensity to import and to take the multiplier as the reciprocal of a fraction equal to the sum of the fraction of marginal income saved and the fraction of marginal income spent on imports. Thus the multiplier was related to the propensity to spend income on home-produced goods. This being so, it is the volume of exports and not the balance of trade that has to be taken as the base of the multiplier. This brings the theory into line with Keynes, particularly with the *General Theory* as distinct from the *Treatise on Money*. In the latter, you remember, it is the excess of investment over saving that is important, whereas in the *General Theory* it is the absolute volume of investment. By like reasoning it should be the absolute volume of exports, not the balance of trade, that is important. If we deal in balances then it is anomalous to take ex-ante values for home saving and investment and ex-post values for the foreign balance (I do not know how one can take ex-ante values for the latter) ; but if one takes ex-post values for both there is never any balance at all, since the excess of ex-post investment over saving is always equal to the excess of imports over exports. In my system the increase in the volume of exports would be rightly found to have a stimulating effect on employment, even although, through consequential reactions in home investment, no addition to the balance of trade ensued.

In my system the balance of trade depends on whether the ratio of the volume of exports to the volume of home investment is greater or less than the ratio of the propensity to import (viz. imports represented as a fraction of income) to the propensity to save. I suggested that there was no *a priori* reason why these ratios should be equal or why therefore foreign trade should stand in neutral balance. The continuance of a negative balance would of course depend on the possibility of getting continued accommodation from abroad to finance it. If such accommodation were not forthcoming, a crisis would occur, including in the old-fashioned world a bank-rate crisis — we do not yet know what form the crisis would take in the new controlled world — and investment would come tumbling down. This would bring an end to the excess of the ratio, propensity to import to propensity to save, over the ratio, volume of exports to volume of home investment. On the other hand there seems to be nothing to check the continuance of a positive balance, save in so far as the progressive accumulation of liquid assets accompanied by falling interest rates may serve to increase the volume of home investment. Whether one would get a sufficient stimulus in that direction would no doubt depend on the elasticity of the marginal productivity of capital. Thus there does seem to be an asymmetry here between the nature of the forces acting upon debit and credit countries respectively, and some justification for the general feeling that the credit countries, in so far as they did not make appropriate plans to invest their balance abroad in real capital projects, were exerting a sort of stranglehold. For this reason I place a high value upon the scarce currency clause in the Bretton Woods Agreement, despite the admitted awkwardness that might occur in the application of it. It is an attempted remedy for a real evil of quite central importance in the world economy. Its value lies not so much in the proposed measures to be taken if a currency were declared scarce, as in throwing the onus of responsibility where it should lie, in bringing to bear upon credit countries a force in the form of a threat, of strength comparable to those forces, which are also in the first instance kinds of threats, that automatically come to bear upon the debit countries.

Now in my handbook I said explicitly that all this analysis was static and would require reconsideration if a dynamic economics were ever developed. How, you may ask, did I deem that it made sense at all to argue in terms of the static analysis when the concepts in question, saving and investment, were so palpably dynamic concepts? I think one may plead that these arguments were not altogether nonsensical, just as one may plead that the *General Theory*, despite its lack of a dynamic property, is not nonsensical. Nonsense is turned into sense, although not into a fully correct analysis, by the basic assumption which, though unjustified, one may use to go on with, that the marginal productivity of capital (which governs the volume of investment) is an external datum, a gift of God, so to speak, a fundamental condition, like tastes and productivity, which determines the values of the dependent variables. The system of thought is dynamized as soon as we regard the schedule of the marginal productivity of capital not as something which is taken as given but as a function of the rate of growth of the economy.

It is with some regret that I have to report that when we take foreign trade into account the fundamental equation has to be written in the form

$$GC = s - b,$$

where b is the balance of trade expressed as a fraction of income. I say that it is with regret that I report this, because one naturally hates to give expression to any form of words which may be used as ammunition by the hateful mercantilists. They are only too ready to seize upon any material and distort it to serve their own purposes. In the long run, however, the right cause cannot but be helped by a more complete understanding. Since this form of expression is distasteful to me, you may imagine that I examined it with the most critical acerbity. I have confidence in its correctness, and the fact that there was, so to speak, no escape from it enhances my confidence in this dynamic equation as a tool of thought. I came to the matter without prejudice (or perhaps with the prejudice on the other side) and the equation provided me with an answer that I could not gainsay.

We may further write

$$G_w C_r = s - b.$$

For a country in which G_w is tending to exceed G_n and

there is by consequence a chronic tendency to depression, a positive value of b may be beneficial. This clearly tends to reduce the value of G_w and might bring it into a better relation to G_n. This proposition is perhaps obvious after all. A country where saving is high in relation to her potentialities of further growth will be helped by opportunity for investment abroad. That is from the country's own point of view. In international policy we shall have to look at the matter from the point of view of other countries also. It is to be noted that the absence of growth, or of sufficient growth, is as important as the level of income and saving in determining whether it is good to have a positive balance.

I am afraid, therefore, that I cannot join with those who urge that a large volume of exports are of no particular value for the United States and particularly that a large unbalanced volume of exports is of no particular value. It may be just these unbalanced exports that are of particular value. There has been a tendency by some to argue that the Americans are foolish to look to pushing exports as a means of getting employment, on the ground that the greatest possible value that one can imagine for her exports would still be small in relation to her national income and her unemployment potential and therefore would not be an important factor helping her to full employment. This is altogether to neglect the multiplier effect of such exports. And I think it is clear that the multiplier effect is stronger the longer the view that one takes.

Next it is necessary to set out formulae for the growth of exports. Let $_eG$ stand for the rate of growth of exports and E for the value of exports; let $_hG$ stand for the rate of growth of output for the home market and H for the value of that output. Let $_hG_w$ stand for the warranted rate of growth of output for the home market. Then

$$\frac{_eGE \cdot {_h}GH}{E+H} \cdot C = GC = s,$$

$$\frac{_eGE \cdot {_h}G_wH}{E+H} \cdot C_r = G_wC_r = s.$$

If the rate of growth of exports exceeds the rate of growth of production for the home market, then the rate of growth of exports will exceed the total rate of growth. If the rate of growth of exports exceeds the warranted rate of growth for the home market, then the rate of growth of exports will exceed the total warranted growth, and the warranted rate of growth of production for the home market will be less than the total warranted rate of growth. In these conditions, with the propensity to import constant, b will grow through time. This will tend to reduce the warranted total rate of growth, and thus, if initially the warranted total rate of growth is above the natural rate of growth, will tend to bring the former into line with the latter. If in these circumstances the rate of growth of exports continued to be in excess of the warranted rate of total growth, we should have a tendency towards inflationary conditions. Then (but I fear then only) could we begin to expostulate with the Americans that their export drive was doing them no good.

It may be interesting to note in passing that if our problem is the trade cycle one, the runaway of actual growth downwards from the warranted rate, an increase in the volume of exports in and by itself will have a restorative tendency, whether the balance of trade is thereby improved or not. In cases where the increase of exports stimulates home investment, the net effect may be a less favourable balance of trade, but this would not at all reduce the restorative effect of the increase of exports — just the contrary.

But when we look at the long-period problem, the failure of the natural rate to be as high as the warranted rate, then it is an improvement of the balance of trade that is needed as a corrective. Thus in the context of cyclical trade depression the doctrine of my *International Economics*, that it is the volume not the balance of exports that matters, is correct, and the doctrine of the *Treatise* is misleading. But in the context of the long-period problem the doctrine of the *Treatise* comes into its own. This may be another example of Keynes having a correct hunch before he had made the analysis necessary to justify it. It cannot be claimed that there is any such analysis in the *Treatise*.

What is likely to determine the rate of growth of exports? Three governing principles may be mentioned. Of these much the most important is the rate of growth of the foreign economy as a whole. If this exceeds the rate of growth of the domestic economy, then, other things being equal, the balance of trade will increase. This is the most easy and natural way for it to increase. The home country has merely to retain its proportionate share of foreign markets. Under this head the American balance might be expected to decline, which is inconvenient for her. In the battle of accusations between the United States and the rest of the world, the former is arraigned for her tendency to severe slump, which has unfavourable reactions throughout the world. She might reply that it is precisely because the rest of the world is so relatively stagnant that she tends to have recurrent slumps! All one-sided accusations are no doubt very foolish.

Secondly, we must have regard to our old friend,

never out of date and never to be despised, the law of comparative costs. If the rate of growth of output per head in the products in which a country has comparative advantage exceeds the rate of growth of her national income, then the rate of growth of her exports will tend to exceed her total rate of growth and the balance of trade will tend to increase. This was no doubt the governing factor in the course of British trade in the time following the industrial revolution. It is not enough for a country to be more progressive than others for her balance of trade to grow; on the contrary, the fact that she is more progressive will in itself tend to make her balance of trade sink; she must be more progressive in the lines in which she already has the lead, than she is in other lines.

Finally there is the relation between the rate of growth in the rewards to factors of production other than profit, in terms of tradable goods, to the rate of growth of output per head. If the ratio between these rates is one, then this determinant is neutral, and the rate of growth of the balance of trade will be governed by the other two forces only. If the ratio is less than one, then the balance of trade will tend to grow, subject to the condition that its growth as so determined does not pull the warranted rate of growth of the economy below its natural rate.

Understanding of this may be facilitated by reference to static analysis. If contractual (non-profit) rewards to factors are fixed too high, a country will suffer from unemployment. The number of lines in which her costs are such as to allow her to offer them at competitive prices abroad is restricted, and the number of lines in which she has to surrender the home market or part of it to foreigners increased. The law of comparative costs still operates; but the range of goods that can be offered with mercantile advantage is restricted, the range of goods that can be bought abroad with mercantile advantage being correspondingly increased, while owing to low employment (and income) the volume of the latter is restricted, precisely so as to offset their greater range, and there is equilibrium at a low level of trade and employment. According to the old ideas this would not be a position of equilibrium, since gold would flow out or the foreign exchange rates be depressed forcing gold rewards to factors down. We now discard this notion. Keynes's theory that equilibrium with unemployment may be stable in certain circumstances of investment opportunity and saving was extended in my *International Economics* to apply by similar reasoning to unemployment due to too high a rate of rewards in relation to the foreign trade position.

If rewards were lower, there would be more employment; if sufficiently low, " full employment "; if they were lower still (as, some say, in Japan) there would not be still more employment, but profit inflation; a reduction of wages in all occupations below the " full employment " level would not have any further tendency to stimulate experts; profits being inflated, exports would be restricted to the range shown by the law of comparative costs, it being possible to make still higher profits in the rest of the field by selling in the home market.

These static principles have their analogues in dynamics. If rewards to factors generally do not rise as rapidly as output per man, the range of goods that can be sold abroad with mercantile advantage will grow for this reason; exports will tend to grow more rapidly than national income and therefore the balance of trade will tend to grow. But, as in the static analysis, there is a limiting condition. If the balance grows, it can be seen from the equation that the warranted rate of growth of the economy is pulled down; if this is pulled below the natural rate there will be a chronic tendency to inflationary conditions, and these, by a similar principle to that of the static analysis, will restrict the growth of exports and prevent a further increase in the balance of trade. Thus the rate of growth of a country's productive potential has a decisive effect in restricting the growth in her balance of trade.

Those who fear a rising deluge of American goods in the world markets should discipline their thoughts by reference to these principles. If the United States continues to be more progressive than the average of countries, that it itself will be a force tending to reduce her balance; her imports will grow more quickly than her export outlets. The other two forces will only cause a rising balance to the extent that they can more than offset this primary force. To what extent is the increase of efficiency in the United States in producing the types of goods which she exports likely to exceed her increase of efficiency generally? And to what extent is the average increase in real rewards to factors (other than profit takers) likely to fall short of the average increase of output per head?

It is true that an American administration with a full employment plan might endeavour to overcome the natural obstacles to achieving a sufficient export surplus by differential subsidies for exports. That business subsidizes exports by an appropriate distribution of overheads is of course well recognized. But to make the rate of growth of exports greater than that determined by natural forces it would probably be necessary for these subsidies to be progressively increased through time. If we regard an undue pressure by the Americans to export as a danger, then we should do well to enter into agreements limiting the scope of official export subsidies.

This is in fact another reason for pressing on with the kind of international code of good behaviour envisaged in Article 7 of the Mutual Aid Agreement and recent discussions. We thereby no doubt deprive ourselves of the weapon of export subsidies. This may seem a weapon to which we shall be absolutely driven by the present exigencies. We must not allow ourselves to develop a panicky attitude about the present situation. I suggest in that connexion that either our balance will, despite the immediate signs to the contrary, come right, or that, if it does not do so, a far more radical treatment of our economic problem than the mere provision of export subsidies will be indicated as necessary. Subsidies to exports might do positive harm in further postponing the need for such a radical overhaul.

If we take a longer period, it is surely clear that from the full employment point of view — and that point of view is likely to have a paramount influence on policy — our need for a high rate of growth of exports is likely to be much less than the American. Consequently their tendency to have mounting subsidies for exports, if these are allowed, is likely to be stronger than anything we should seek, save in competition with theirs. From our point of view it would certainly be better to outlaw competition in the granting of export subsidies.

How, it may be asked, do British exporting prospects stand in the light of this analysis? Unfortunately this problem, so much the most important for us, has no connexion with the analysis of trends; for the British problem is that of a large once-over change in the level of her exports. But we must beware of ambiguity in this term " once-over ". We require a large once-over change in the annual level of our exports, and this, of course, cannot be met by a mere once-over demand for a set of goods by other countries to meet re-stocking needs. It would take me too far from my subject to scrutinize the prospects of her achieving this once-over change without a serious once-over deterioration in her standard of living.[1] I will only mention that a large movement towards greater freedom of trade would be of paramount value.

In the long run it would probably be appropriate for Britain to have some positive balance. Her stationary population within a world of rising population will be a force tending to offset what we hope will be a superior progressiveness in output per head and to facilitate an increase in her balance. The prospective increase of world efficiency, if this takes effect in consequence of international plans, will work in two opposite ways for Britain; the growth of markets will tend to raise her exports, but the growth of efficiency in manufacturing industry may tend to reduce the scope of the gain which accrues to her under the law of comparative costs.

We may now take the world scene. We have to ask the question whether for the world as a whole the war-ranted rate of growth is greater or less than the natural rate. It would be rash to dogmatize. The inter-war doldrums suggested that the warranted rate was unduly high. In many parts, of course, saving was painfully absent, but so also was improvement in production. There may be an excess of saving in one part and a lack of growth in another simply owing to the absence of capital in the latter. Thus we would not get the picture of de-pression in the over-saving parts and a tendency to inflation in the remainder, but merely stagnation in the remainder. A revival of the international movement

---

[1] This has been admirably done in an article by Mr. G. D. A. Mac-Dougall in the *Economic Journal*, March 1947.

of capital may assist the natural rate of growth. It is assumed that the international movement of capital will be accompanied by an international movement of " know how ".

It may be well to enumerate the difficulties, which are well known, that confront a large-scale international movement. In the first place, and this is probably the most important point of all, there are vast regions to which the old classical analysis still applies, the regions in which population is pressing upon the means of subsistence. Fertilize these with new capital and the population merely expands. If these regions were at present relatively under-populated, one might take one's chance, hoping that, as in the case of the more advanced regions, one might succeed in getting production temporarily to outstrip population increase, getting thereby a better standard of living and, as a consequence, an effect upon the birth-rates. But what does the time lag involve? If it were anything like that which applied in Western Europe in the last century, the intervening increase of population would be fatally large, having regard to the already over-populated state of these backward regions. Does it not almost seem that we will have to tackle the birth-rate question as a prior condition of any really large capital outlay in those regions?

Secondly, there is the political question of the desir-ability of growing financial dependence of certain parts of the world on one or two rich countries. The Inter-national Bank may help here, but only if it is international in fact as well as in name—and is that possible? It would certainly be very important for this country quite boldly to seek to play a leading rôle in the Bank — despite her lack of any immediate prospect of making large contribu-tions to its resources — if only this country was in a mood to take her international economic responsibilities seriously. How can she be, it might be argued, with her own house in such disorder? That is a pity. All the same there are two sides to the question. It is possible that if she addressed herself with more earnestness to these long-range international problems, she would be forced to think of her own problems in a way that might suggest better solutions of them.

Thirdly, allied to this political question, is the risk of default. This itself, as it seems to me, depends on the extent to which an international welding together by the enlargement of trade and the successful operation of joint international institutions proceeds, or how far we are to lapse ever further into the autarkic point of view.

Finally there is the problem of service and redemption. Here it must be admitted that the United States will have in the long run to solve her own problem otherwise than by a continued expansion of her balance of trade. This brings us back to the main question. What, for a country or for the world as a whole, is the proper solution if there is a persistent tendency for the warranted rate of growth to stand above the natural rate?

Before giving our final consideration to this problem we must revert to that of the shorter period, particularly the trade cycle.

(b) CONTRA-CYCLICAL POLICY

Our considerations have given good grounds, and there are others, for regarding the trade cycle as likely to continue.

1. First and foremost is the instability of any possible steady line of advance as revealed by the fundamental equations. Total output being the resultant of numerous

decisions, many of them based on uncertain data, we can hardly expect it to conform to the level required by the steady line of advance. But we have seen that any divergences on either side of this line take output into a field in which it is drawn farther and farther from the line. It would not be right to present this as a complete theory of the trade cycle; it merely displays a framework within which a detailed theory of the cycle should be worked out.

2. Even if fundamental conditions were broadly subject only to steadily continuing change, divergences from the steady line, and thereby extended movements away from it, would be likely owing to minor miscalculations. But fundamental conditions are not likely to be steady. For instance, inventions may be expected to follow the wayward course of genius. From time to time we may get a crop of labour-saving inventions outweighing the effect of those of a capital-saving character. If these came, for instance, at a time when the system had been progressing steadily on its warranted line, they would pull down the value of G_w. G would be hardly likely to adapt itself at once. There is an analogy here with Wicksell's concept of the divergence of the actual from the natural rate of interest being due more often to a change in the former than to any misguided attempt by the bankers to change the latter, the banks being deemed by him to maintain existing procedures under the influence of *vis inertiae*. According to the formulation I have given, additional capital outlay due to the labour-saving character of the inventions would be included in d on the right-hand side of the equation. By some adjustment of definitions they could alternatively be included in C_r, thus enlarging it. In either case the effect on G_w is the same, namely to reduce it, and put it below the actual

rate. And so we should go off into a vicious spiral of expansion.

3. It has been suggested that in pursuit of the objective of a steadily falling rate of interest over the long period, in practice we may have to proceed by bumps, and these are likely to have the same effect as other exogenous shocks in twisting the economy away from its steady line of advance.

4. Although I have not dealt with them, I have little doubt that our lag experts are right in thinking that various lags, inseparable from a system in which decisions have to be based on imperfect data and to some extent therefore on trial and error, are likely to set up a cycle.

5. There is no need to treat as *vieux jeux* many of the theories advanced to demonstrate the likelihood of a movement, once started, developing an cumulative character. I refer to theories in the field of money and of psychology. These still have their part to play.

What are the remedies? I think that we are now in a position to record and ask for endorsement for a negative point of cardinal importance. It seems clear that variations in the rate of interest will not play an important part in our contra-cyclical armoury. This certainly follows from the argument of these lectures and is, I think, implicit in much recent writing. And in practice this weapon has now been discarded for fifteen years. Practical men might say that economists were a little tardy in their discoveries.

So much discussion, however, of contra-cyclical policy has for generations concentrated upon interest rate policy, that this conclusion, if I am right in deeming that it is a final conclusion, constitutes a major revolution in this field, and is, therefore, worth dwelling upon. Discarding the interest-rate cure or relegating it to a position of secondary importance means, I suppose, discarding the monetary cure in the form in which it has been traditionally advanced. It is possible that there may still be room for some other kind of monetary cure, of which I shall have something to say. It is also possible that short-term interest-rate policy may yet serve some useful subordinate rôle, *e.g.* in checking speculation, if only our long-term interest-rate policy allows us to take such liberties with the short-term rate. It may not do so.

The great exponent of the short-term rate has been for so long Mr. Hawtrey. His pen is persuasive, his views are constructive and would be most welcome, if only we could believe them. That the short-term rate has been most potent in British banking history is obvious enough. The field in which its aid was most urgently needed and in which its quick effects were undoubted and decisive was that of the short-term foreign balance of payments. About its efficacy in that respect there is no dispute. It has also been used to break the boom at the top. But that is a very different matter from curbing a boom or reducing a recession in the earlier stages of either. It may also have had effects through its influence on the long-term rate or on psychology. That again is a different matter. The proposition now under consideration, the characteristically Hawtrey proposition, is that a variation in the short-term rate tends to have a direct effect on the volume of activity by making it more or less profitable to hold additional stocks (whether of raw materials or semi-finished goods). The chorus of merchants and traders and producers have testified in the negative. Not a single Hawtreyite is to be found in the world of practical men. The theorist only has to dot the i's and cross the t's. He may point out that where goods are of the homogeneous character and can be dealt with in an organized exchange, or near it, risks of price fluctuation within a short period are very large compared with possible variations in the short-term rate of interest for a short period, *e.g.* one quarter of the variations in the short-term rate per annum. The speculator, or the producer or trader who ventures to hold stocks additional to his most convenient requirements, is boldly pitting his view against the market view; where the risk is so great, if he acts in this way, he is likely to be rather strongly of his opinion and to foresee, according to his notion, a sizable profit. When bracing himself up to this decision with all its implications, he is not likely to weigh the plus or minus half per cent of interest. Where the goods are less standardized and more finished, obsolescence at once becomes a danger. Again the risk of holding redundant stock is considerable. Nor, on the other hand, can he let his stocks fall below his convenient requirements. In ordinary times, unlike ours, a trader or producer who cannot meet his customer's order in a line in which he specializes, for lack of stock-in-hand, must look rather a fool and suffer loss of good will. He will hardly run the risk of this for the sake of the plus or minus half per cent.

And the long-term rate? Here there are two points of which I reserve the more important for the second place. Doubts have been expressed about the elasticity of the demand for capital. We have the elegant article on this subject by Mr. Shackle in the March issue of the *Economic Journal*, 1946. I will not repeat his arguments. It is possible that this is one of those cases where demand (and perhaps supply also) responds rather slowly to a change in price, and that if we look at the increase in the demand for long-term capital during a decade following a certain reduction in the long-term rate of interest, we might find considerably more responsiveness than we detect by considering only what may happen in the following few months. I shall have to return to this point when I come finally round to the long-term problem. But this does not help us with our trade cycle problem. What we there want is responsiveness preferably within a few months, but, at the very worst, within a year or two. Longer range responsiveness does not help us. One dare not dogmatize, but I am inclined to attach weight to the views of those who urge us not to expect a very great increase of capital outlay in the period immediately following a change in the long-term rate of interest.

The more important point in connection with the long-term rate is that it will in no wise be possible for us to make this rate move up and down by substantial amounts within the ambit of the cycle. If this were a declared policy it would at once defeat itself. Who would mark some Government Stock up to 150 when it was the known intention of the monetary authorities to force it down to 100 within a trade-cycle period? We might expect such a policy to effect changes amounting to a fraction of 1 per cent, and these are the sorts of changes that have in fact occurred in the past. But, manifestly, we cannot expect to show quick responsiveness in plans for long range capital outlay to such minute changes. Larger changes are out of the question. The one spectacular change in the long-term rate, other than in war, was that effected by Chamberlain in 1932, but this was based on a general opinion that after three years of profitless industry the time was ripe for a return — a permanent return, mark you — to our historic 3 per cent. What is left of the interest rate as a contra-cyclical weapon?

What then of other remedies? I do not think that public works should also be regarded as altogether outmoded, especially if we can widen this concept to include all forms of capital outlay that may be subject to influence, direct or indirect, by the central authority. There are certainly most difficult problems of timing. Much has still to be done in the way of the spread of enlightenment and of change in administrative procedure before the local authorities will pull their full weight in co-operating on such a contra-cyclical policy. No doubt the same applies to the semi-public concerns and other important spending bodies that may eventually be subject to influence. Our problems are such at the moment that, despite the White Paper of the Coalition Government, we are hardly beginning yet to see any such influence exerted.

There is a large field here for international co-operation, not only through the actual operations of the International Bank, but also by getting international machinery for mutual consultation with the purpose of synchronizing those variations in outlay which the various nations are able to finance through their own resources. There is no reason to suppose that the United States would not be interested in proposals for synchronizing some of her domestic projects in conformity with a properly agreed world contra-cyclical policy endorsed by the best experts. In countries which have housing subsidies, these surely could and should be used to iron out the building cycle, which has been of such large amplitude. At present I fear that we here are moving in the exactly opposite direction, and by toying with house demolition plans of fabulous dimensions are making a slump in the building industry worse than any known in that or any other industry quite inevitable at the end of a decade. We should remember that with the impending stationary population a very great shrinkage in our building industry will be required, and we should spread our house demolition plans over a reasonably long term of years, so as to get the building industry to move more or less steadily down to that lower level which is inevitable in the long run.

Then we have the ten-year Budget. The greater the difficulties, and they may well be considerable, of adjusting the timing of large capital outlay to fit in with the requirements of a contra-cyclical policy the more we may have to rely on variations in the Budget. Deficit spending is a tap that can be turned on quickly, and the most welcome way of turning it on is to reduce taxation. We certainly do not want public works which are merely thought up as a means for spending money. It will, alas, be many a long year before we can afford such a luxury in this country, and in any case it is a silly luxury. Much better to reduce taxes and allow the citizens to spend this happy windfall. And, if they do not spend it, the taxes can be reduced still further! Variations in the Budget deficit appeared to have a potent short-term influence in the United States in the 'thirties. This form of contra-cyclical policy could also become the subject of international co-operation, Budget deficits and surpluses being synchronized — at least by the more responsible governments! — in accordance with the finding of experts on the appropriate international body.

It has for some time appeared to me that we require a third contra-cyclical weapon, namely a plan for government financed buffer stocks. The other inflationary taps may not tend to create demand in those sectors of the economy which are most exposed to the blast of depression. Yet, if we are indeed dealing with a mere tidal ebb and not a permanent recession of the waters, it is not desirable that the personnel should be shifted away from their site or trade when they will be wanted back there in full numbers after two or three years. It should be possible to make a catalogue of what are some times called bread-and-butter lines in the various industries, to which redundant personnel in a depression could be turned over. Firms do this of course to some extent on their own account, producing for stock, but they cannot carry the process far enough. It should be possible to find a sufficient number and variety of goods belonging to the different centres of industry that could be held in stock without danger of obsolescence during the slump period. To help the British economy the list must include, and indeed must mainly consist of, processed articles. Particular regard should be had to items which may give alternative employment to those affected by a recession in our export markets. Of course it will be necessary to be very objective in the execution of this policy lest positions liable to secular obsolescence are protected on the false pretext of being merely the victims of a transitional trade-cycle phase.

Plans for international buffer stocks have been under discussion for some years. These, of course, need, in the first instance, to be confined to primary products. They have been on the agenda of the Food and Agriculture Organization and of the International Trade Organization. The former body appears to have abandoned the idea of a full international plan, and to have proposed that authority should be delegated to the national governments to act separately. I hope that this may be reconsidered. Perhaps the International Trade Organization will come to the rescue of the more comprehensive and hopeful idea.

In the discussions in the Food and Agriculture Organization attention appears to have been focused on the plan near the heart of that champion of the distressed,

Sir John Boyd Orr, for distributing surpluses to the needy. I have already given expression to my somewhat Malthusian qualms about that particular expedient as a continuing policy. But whatever good might come of it, I judge that it would be small by comparison with the great universal benefits that would flow from a really effective piece of contra-cyclical machinery dealing with primary products. It seems to me that the buffer stock plan is the most potent weapon for dealing with world slump on an international scale that has yet been discussed. And are we not right to think very strenuously about that world slump? It has become the fashion in this country to talk always about the American slump. That is rather rude, and unscientific, and not conducive to the right kind of thinking on this subject. It is probably true that the United States is likely to be the first great nation to encounter a post-war slump. That is not the same as saying that it is always most likely to be the original source of future world slumps. That may be true, or it may not be. It may be true that the United States was the source of the world slump of 1929–32. Or it may not be. Another view is that the true source of that was a world-wide maladjustment in the position of primary products, which preceded the American slump by an ample margin of time, and that America was merely the first victim of forces emanating from this world-wide maladjustment. It may also be true that if we could define effective international measures for checking the course of a world-wide slump at an early phase we might incidentally check the American slump. The exact inter-relations between a possible American slump and a world slump are most worthy of study, but it is begging very many questions to assume a causal rôle for America in every case, and also to assume that the right remedy necessarily lies inside America. I think that part of international co-operation should consist in reaching and promulgating the best views about what the several nations should do on their own account in the face of a slump, whether world-wide or their own, and that such information should be conveyed to the Americans, and that they would be interested in it and quite possibly carry that interest into action. But alongside of that we have also to consider what may be regarded as world-wide action in relation to a world-wide slump. And this brings me back to the buffer stocks scheme. The issues at stake in this question of handling a world slump are portentous for the survival of freedom and the maintenance of peace. The lives of millions, both of those distressed now and also of the young and hopeful now — and we should not forget them — may depend on its success. And I therefore say quite frankly that I put the potential benefit of the contra-cyclical operation of buffer stocks very much higher than Sir John Boyd Orr's scheme.

There are certain principles which ought to be laid down for the conduct of international buffer stocks. The first principle, of course, is that prices should be held steady or fairly steady as depression deepens. This involves in some sense of the word guaranteed prices. Thereby the incomes of a large sector of the world economy would be sustained, and their purchasing power sustained. If this were done, I believe that the vicious spiral of depression could be, and indeed must, by consequence, be broken. I do not see how the process of a general fall in prices and employment could proceed far in a vicious spiral if so many important prices and such a large sector of incomes were being sustained.

Secondly, and equally important—for without this the scheme would speedily crumble — prices must be adjusted in the long run to an economic level, that is to a level at which supply and demand balance without restriction of output. This may mean in many cases that prices will have to fall over a term of years, and that many high cost producers will have to be squeezed out. This may be in some senses a painful process, but it will be essential if the world is to make economic progress. And the pain of it will be greatly mitigated by the gradualness of the decline. The high-cost producers will have due notice, some years of notice, that the world market is moving ineluctably against them, and that unless they can radically alter their costs they must move to another occupation. The governments of countries like Bolivia, too dependent on a single commodity, will have due notice, and should take suitable measures within the philosophy of international co-operation to diversify their production.

I suggest that in order to reconcile the first and second of these basic principles there should be, so to speak, an overriding standing order that a buffer stock shall never in one year alter its buying price by more than 3 per cent. It may seem odd to mention a particular figure in a fundamental principle; it may be that this figure is not quite right; perhaps it should be $2\frac{1}{2}$ or 2 per cent. But the right figure cannot be very far from my figure if we are to combine the principle of sustaining income during the slump with the principle of working towards the economic price in the long run.

To implement its task of keeping the price steady, yet without allowing restriction schemes, which should be taboo save in very special circumstances, each stock must be prepared to buy without limit of quantity. In this it should be in exactly the same position as a central bank operating a gold standard.

It should establish buying and selling prices — also like the bank — but in this case probably some 20 per cent apart, to allow for the free working of commodity markets, and to provide anyhow the possibility of covering its storage costs. It must be faced, however, that some part of these costs might have to be carried by interested parties — by producer and consumer nations presumably in proportion to their interest — as a payment for the great benefits likely to flow from the scheme.

Unlimited buying at a price is essential to effective contra-cyclical achievement. Agricultural experts are apt to take alarm, foreseeing a deluge of production and mounting surpluses being offered for purchase. But the complement of unlimited buying should be an ineluctable long-run downward price movement, slow but steady, should a stock show a tendency to grow in good and bad years alike. And it is absurd to suppose that this would not ultimately eliminate redundant production.

Agriculturists tend to prefer limited buying as more practicable. If this is to be consistent with price maintenance through a recession it must entail restriction; in years of trade recession the restriction would have to be intensified or the price reduced. Such a policy, though relieving producers of part of their troubles in a slump, is not genuinely contra-cyclical.

Likewise agriculturists do not relish the prospect of a long-period downward trend. This is not at all the philosophy, for instance, of the American " parity " principle. Hence a soft spot for the Boyd Orr scheme, which seems to open a door to indefinite price maintenance. A broader humanity sees virtue in cheaper food for all, not for restricted classes of needy persons only; the great majority of people in the world are not so comfortable that they would not be relieved of much pain by having food available at lower prices. Agriculturists do not like to recognize the plain truth that wide sectors of the population must be shooed away from food production, if the world is to progress. This follows from the limited capacity of the human stomach and the law that man spends a smaller fraction of his income on primary products as he advances. Agriculturists would prefer to spread the required production from a given agricultural population, taken as more or less fixed; but this would be a bar to progress.

It does not help their case to cite the vast and widespread under-nourishment that now exists. For that increase of consumption which we hope those sectors will achieve must be balanced, unless they are to be the objects of permanent charity, by a corresponding increase in their production — of something.

While it may be pointed out to the agriculturists that a reduction in the oscillation of prices, with the increased short- and medium-term security which that offers, would be of very great benefit to agricultural producers, yet the buffer-stock policy must not be shaped to favour any sectional interests, but to be of general benefit. Plans for buffer stocks of the kind most often discussed are still rather far removed from contra-cyclical policy. A revolution of thought is required. Conquest of the trade cycle will not be achieved without it.

In my final lecture I shall return to the long-range problem.

IS INTEREST OBSOLETE?

AND so finally we come to the long-range problem. Here we have to advance cautiously, tentatively. If one contemplates, as one should, far-reaching possibilities, this should not imply a dogmatic affirmation that one can see here and now any particular solution to be necessary. But it is valuable to acclimatize one's mind to the atmosphere of bold plans. I think that we have been proceeding by the method of patchwork too long, and that the inconveniences of attempting to solve one's problems without regard to principle are even now in the process of becoming apparent.

Will conditions in Britain be such, when the transition is over, as to require a steadily falling rate of interest? Will they be such in the United States? What is necessary there to-day may be necessary here to-morrow. May one think that over there temper is not altogether averse from a far-reaching experiment, provided always that it is conformable to the fundamental philosophy of political and economic freedom?

Our reasoning has shown that a falling rate of interest is much more likely to be required when the population is stationary. The sinister possibility of a declining population cannot be left out of account, even of one declining rather rapidly. If, as may well be the case, saving is a function not only of the size of income but of the volume of accumulated outstanding titles to future income, then the existence of a large dead-weight debt is a force making for a redundancy of saving. In my fundamental equation (Lecture 3) saving was represented as a constant fraction of income ; this was only an *ad hoc* expedient ; it may well also be a function of the volume of private capital. This would not affect the general argument which I developed from the fundamental equation.

If we could optimistically contemplate a growth of output per head as high as $1\frac{1}{2}$ per cent a year, which appears to be somewhat above experience, capital requirements $(G_n C_r)$ might be about 6 per cent of income. Even this may be too high, since it assumes the marginal capital coefficient to be of the same order of magnitude as the present over-all capital coefficient, but marginal accretions to income in our present phase may well be spent on valuables of a primarily service character, on cinemas and dog-racing if you will, for which the marginal capital coefficient is lower than the over-all coefficient. This would reduce requirements below 6 per cent of income. This points strongly to the necessity for a falling rate of interest. I always have in mind that in the great era of expansion in Britain the population increase alone probably entailed a requirement for saving of some 6 per cent of income and that another sizable fraction went away in overseas investment. With these sources of demand for capital cut off, the former irretrievably in Britain for a number of decades, there is a strong *a priori* presumption that saving will tend to redundancy. This provides a cogent reason for not regarding the speculations that are to follow as merely academic. In this long-range survey we must set our minds free from thoughts about the immediate pressures arising from great schemes of modernizing British industry and rehousing. With population stationary a great reduction tending to an elimination of the requirement of new capital for building of all sorts is inevitable. And if we really go in for Americanizing British industry, this, once it is done, is likely to be adverse to the elongation of the production process. It is the old British not the American technique that requires long-lived machinery; on the American plan machinery is tending ever towards becoming the direct cost of current output rather than a charge that has to be amortized over a number of years.

What is likely to be the value of the increase of capital required per unit of output d, if the interest rate is constant? I see no reason to believe that it is likely to be positive; I cannot dogmatize, but merely throw this out as a challenge to the statisticians. Of course if d were substantially positive this might help.

There has been much discussion recently of redistribution of income as a method of reducing the propensity to save. On this economists clearly cannot, and ought not, to have the last word. This is a matter most central for the consideration of political scientists, if only there was any political science. I believe that there are deep laws relating the distribution of power (money is power) to the stability of a political organism. Economists are entitled to rush in with expostulations about incentive. They may cite Russia where, despite the creed of socialism, a very unequal distribution appears to be deemed necessary, though not necessarily correctly so, for the maintenance of incentive.

There is another point about which we must be cautious. It is quite possible that the Americans can go further towards damping saving by means of redistribution than we now can. As the number of rich people with money to hand declines there may be a strong stimulus to corporate saving. And as wage-earners rise to a level at which prudence is possible, we may expect massive saving on that side. I leave this question open.

We now come to a crucial matter, long deferred. What about the elasticity of the demand for capital? What about the prospect of getting a substantial elongation, a good positive value for d, through a falling rate of interest? Scepticism on this point is growing. I have already referred to the demonstration provided by Mr. Shackle in his article in the *Economic Journal* in March 1946. I hasten to add that there may be a very big difference between the effect of a fall in interest in a fairly short period, such as the trade-cycle period, and in a much longer period. The former point is important as regards the possibility of ironing out the cycle by means of changes in the long-term rate of interest. While the fall in this rate may not produce any strong immediate effect by making entrepreneurs reconsider their productive methods or by making durable goods more attractive to the consumer, it is not inconsistent with this to hold that in due time, that is after there has been time for the lower rate to sink in and become part of the furniture of the mind of entrepreneurs and others, the various adjustments consequent upon it may add up to a sizable amount. This may seem, by the way, to be introducing, contrary to my self-denying ordinance, a time-lag. It would be so if we were now considering the trade cycle. But where you get a steady movement, a lag has no meaning. If the rate of interest falls steadily over an ample period, it does not matter whether the decisions to make production more roundabout at time, t_2, are caused by the fall in interest at t_1 or t_2, both being assumed to be the same in amount. Therefore I would not rule out the possibility that the absorption of saving by elongation in response to a falling rate may be substantial. But I must beg leave to have serious doubts. Cassel referred to an inexhaustible demand for capital if there were no price for it; there is no such inexhaustible demand. We always have to consider amortisation. Is there really a vast mass of installation, confidently expected to pay its own amortisation, if only the rate of interest was $1\frac{1}{2}$ per cent rather than $2\frac{1}{2}$? I crave leave to doubt it. I doubt if a zero rate of interest would produce a revolution in our productive methods. Even in the fruitful field of housing, where the rate of interest may have a substantial effect upon the economic rent — but what does the economic rent matter in these days? — it is important to remember that the rent itself is only a small part of the costs which people have in mind in deciding whether to have a larger or a smaller house. There are the costs of servicing it, heating it, furnishing it, maintaining it. Why, it often happens that people will pay a higher rent for a smaller house of the same quality.

It is sometimes hinted that at zero interest there might be a vast number of permanent installations, which, since they have no amortisation, would then become literally costless, or, strictly, would then only cost their maintenance. There are, I suggest, no such permanent installations. What is there that does not depend on our way of life, our technology, our mode of civilization? Who can say what the face of England will be like in a hundred years, or what particular piece of installation will have a positive value at that time? The population, for one thing, may be almost extinct. What changes in our methods may not be caused by nuclear energy? What of the towns? May not the great mass of people wish to revert to country life, if this is rendered possible by our technical revolutions? Or may they possibly be driven underground by more sinister forces, in the way described many years ago by Mr. E. M. Forster? Or may they live with H. G. Wells suspended in mid-air? I suggest that some amortization must be charged against any man-made equipment.

Of course a very low rate of interest, approaching zero, might have a strong effect on saving. This is a most intriguing question. We simply do not know the answer. According to my analysis " hump saving " should be down, but not necessarily saving for heirs, and corporate saving should be up. Saving might still be more than G_nC_r.

There is no simple means of extrapolating for a continued fall in the rate of interest, and we shall be driven to the expedient of trial and error. How is the trial to be judged as we proceed with it?

It is important not to forget that we shall continue to be beset with the trade cycle problem. In some respects this will complicate matters, but in some respects it may, paradoxically enough, be of assistance. In principle all remedies addressed to dealing with the trade cycle as such should be self-liquidating. What is spent in the bad years should be regained in the good years. Buffer stocks, for instance, must be held in balance in the long run. We cannot let these grow without limit; we cannot let valuable articles run to waste. One must remember that if buffer stocks are to be on a scale adequate to have a potent effect on the trade cycle, they will have to be large. The amount of coffee burnt was by comparison trifling with what these ought to be. Therefore there must be no question of getting into a position in which the goods held cannot be finally consumed. Similarly with the Government deficit. The idea of a ten-year Budget implies that what is over-spent in bad years is offset by surpluses in good years. Some writers have tried to belittle the burden of a mounting interest charge, but this is very dangerous if we have to contemplate a falling population; and surely we cannot acquiesce in such an unsound principle as saddling the posterity of tax-payers with interest payments for our current consumption. Heaven forfend that we should be driven from principle to find sufficient public works to absorb the Government deficit! That would be a monstrous waste of resources which we are not likely to be able to afford in the foreseeable future.

I have always believed that if the trade-cycle remedies are to be effective, we have to be prepared to carry them *à l'outrance*. A limited purchase of grain, a loan to buttress up some unsound position, a Tennessee Valley project — I do not believe that the amounts of these *ad hoc* expedients added together will ever solve the problem. They do not provide a basis of confidence. There is always the question, what happens when they run out? As I see it, the trade-cycle remedy should be so devised that the flow of pump-priming purchasing power is in principle limitless. I think in this connexion of the gold standard, one of the few experiments in economic planning that over many generations was, if you will not allow me to say beneficial, at least successful in achieving what it sought. The essence of the gold standard was that in principle and in practice the authority was prepared to receive gold and to release gold without any limit of quantity. There was no question of saying we will give a certain number of applicants gold or we will vote a certain amount of gold to ease our trade troubles. It was of the essence that gold should be provided absolutely without limit to meet all requirements to the extent of 100 per cent. This in our case was reinforced by the willingness of the central bank to lend on good security at its chosen rate of discount, also absolutely without limit of quantity.

Bagehot has always had a great influence on my thinking in this regard. It was the " without limit of quantity " that was the key to success in any operation of this kind. And I believe that, owing to the essential nature of expectation and uncertainty, this will always be the key to the success of any trade-cycle recipe. Is there a danger that the resolution to carry a supporting programme *à l'outrance* may be sapped by the self-balancing idea? In the case of buffer stocks the authorities should be able to sustain their own resolution by the reflection that, however much they have to buy to support the economy in a slump, in the end their freedom to mark prices down in the long period will enable them to put a stop to unlimited accumulation. I fear that it is impracticable to devise a scheme by which the buffer stocks will be self-liquidating in the sense that they will make no loss at all. Some external finance may be needed to cover part of the cost of storage. But the duty should be laid upon them of securing that in the long run their stocks are cleared.

But what of budget deficits? How far will a Chancellor be willing to go if he is really under most solemn obligation to make these good by surpluses within a ten-year period?

This, I believe, is the point of contact between contra-cyclical policy and long-term policy. And my suggestion is a bold one — but I warned you that we should let our minds range over bold ideas — that debt incurred for the sole purpose of sustaining purchasing power in a slump should carry no interest. Is not this right in principle? Why should money issued, not to create productive assets, but to maintain persons in employment producing goods needed by, freely bought by and consumed by the general public (in consequence of their relief from taxation), carry interest? There is not all that difference between the interest now payable on the floating debt and nothing; but there is a vast gulf of principle.

Once we get away from interest, the maxim of a Ten-year Budget can be relaxed. This relaxation must, however, only be allowed if events, as they develop over a ten-year period, prove that the deepening caused by the falling rate of interest is not sufficient to absorb saving.

I suggest that by using this technique we overcome the necessity for any central authority to form an opinion, which in any case it cannot validly do, on the rate of fall in the rate of interest which is justified by fundamental conditions. If the quantity of new interest-free money accumulates over the years, the market rate of long-term interest will find its own natural way downwards. This will not be a planning decision but the resultant of natural forces. A planning decision is, however, involved, namely about how much deficit to have. We must examine this.

As the rate of interest falls a deepening will occur. We do not know how much deepening or how saving will be effected. We do not know if we shall not have to have a zero rate of interest, or whether even that will produce enough effect on deepening and saving to secure steady progress. It may well be that balance can be achieved at, say, $1\frac{1}{2}$ per cent. It may be at a higher rate or it may be at a lower rate. It would be foolish to try to rush at once to an equilibrium position when we do not know what that is. The expedient of issuing a balancing amount of interest-free debt enables us to feel our way forward. If and in so far as the deepening that occurs as the rate falls is insufficient, that will be made good from time to time and to the required figure by the mopping up of saving in interest-free government paper. Fundamentally this means that what some people save in excess, others, the tax-payers, will consume.

What is to be the criterion of the deficit? We are committed to the principle of " full employment ". I am sure you will agree that it is necessary to have a very guarded definition of this. Taken too literally it might lead to either regimentation or inflation. There are certain circumstances which, I think, should lead us to enlarge our notion of the minimum allowable unemployment percentage. Increased benefits under social security may bring many scrimshankers on to the Register who have hitherto preferred a life of independent poverty. Many members of the submerged tenth have tended to evade the interference involved in reporting to Labour Exchanges, but they may now find themselves compelled to come in. They do not want to work, or only wish to do so occasionally, and it would be an act of barbarism to regiment them. Furthermore, the universalization of Trade Union rates may make it more difficult to give the kind of casual low-grade and low-paid employment which is all that members of this class of people are willing to accept or capable of executing.

We should base ourselves, then, on the proposition that sufficient purchasing power should be issued from time to time to maintain full employment. The amount required to be issued may be expected to vary. Despite all our other devices we may not succeed in preventing some oscillation in the volume of industrial capital outlay ; and exports may oscillate. I have always held that the decision regarding the size of the deficit should not rest with the Chancellor of the Exchequer, who should not be subject to the temptation to have an unbalanced Budget, nor with the Cabinet, which is always under a similar temptation, but with an independent expert Authority. Strictly the Budget would not be unbalanced ; but the yield of taxation would be subvented from time to time by payments into the Exchequer from the Authority, which might be called a Stabilization Fund.

At present there is a tendency to concentrate responsibility for a vast mass of basic decisions affecting economic life upon the government. This will surely be reversed in times to come, socialism or no socialism, because it will become evident that it is inconsistent with democratic control. If the number of diverse decisions which the government has to make becomes too great, it becomes technically impossible for public opinion to bring any sort of influence to bear. In this matter of the Stabilization Fund, Parliament can exert its authority in framing the terms of reference under which it must operate; the terms could be revised from time to time. They would resemble in this the old Bank Charter Acts, save that the Authority would not, of course, be a profit-making body. What it had to do would be clearly set out in the terms of reference, and it would carry on under them, until public opinion required some changes in the terms, which could be properly debated.

The receipts from the Fund would normally go to the relief of taxation. This need not rule out plans for stabilization by varying the volume of Public Works. The department of government responsible for securing the proper timing of public works would operate in close consultation with the Fund. In the matter of correct timing their policies would be similar; but there would also be a great difference between them, namely in their attitude to the total volume of disbursements. Broadly, public works should always be limited in total quantity by regard for economy, only genuinely useful works being undertaken. It is most undesirable that there should be any tendency to view projects with a kindly eye simply on the ground that they would tend to " give employment ". The Stabilization Fund would be under no such inhibition. It would have no qualms as the total of monies issued, save only that they should be of the right amount to maintain " full employment ", however that be defined. Inflation must be avoided.

Although the Fund would normally find it expedient to issue large amounts in times of world or local slump, it would not necessarily have to confine its issue to those periods. That is precisely what will have to be determined by trial and error. That is why I said that the trade cycle may be of positive assistance in framing policy. It establishes an urgent requirement for a Stabilization Fund of this kind ; it calls for tentative and *ad hoc* treatment in its various phases. Each particular issue of money by the Fund would relate to the current phase. There need be no long predetermined policy. Whether, in fact, we shall have a chronic tendency to insufficient demand in the coming years we do not know ; it cannot be predicted. As the fund proceeded with its operations, adjusting them to what was required from time to time, it would gradually become clear whether there was such a tendency. We should find, if events so turned out, that we had made the transition to a long-term policy of sustained subvention to purchasing power. In the years immediately preceding 1929 Lord Keynes was advocating a policy of public works, designed to overcome unemployment, implicitly taken to be abnormal ; and when the world slump came so that the years of 1926–29 in Britain were retrospectively viewed in perspective as years of boom rather than slump, there was a tendency to argue that it was rather absurd of him to have advocated an anti-slump policy at that time. It was not, of course, absurd but perfectly proper. The Stabilization Fund, had it existed then, would have done right to release some purchasing power; then when the slump of 1929-31 came, it should have stepped up its rate of release considerably.

I should make a digression here regarding foreign investment. If this were developed on a large scale it might seriously check the fall in the rate of interest that would otherwise be required. The problem of how much foreign investment this country should undertake in a steadily progressive period of the future should solve itself under the Bretton Woods machinery. I assume that the United States will also be pursuing a policy of falling domestic interest rates, indeed will be ahead in that policy, so that the pull of capital away from Britain in search of higher interest will not be towards the United States but towards other countries where capital is less certainly secure. If interest rates remain higher in other countries, this may be no more than a truly assessed risk premium. Rates on foreign investment have always been much higher than rates obtainable here, but this has not entailed any devastating flight of capital from this country. The risk was judged to be high, and so indeed it has proved. The interest charge on loans guaranteed or made by the International Bank would presumably follow the United States rate downwards, remaining slightly above it. This need not lead to an excessive movement, since the necessity to pay amortization limits the power of other countries to absorb capital whatever the rate of interest.

If the volume of foreign investment by Britain remains under control, the Stabilization Fund would no doubt act in concert with the department of the Treasury exerting that control and with the International Bank. Setting up such a Fund would be a notable contribution to the policy of maintaining full employment at home, which members of the International Trade Organization are under obligation to endeavour to implement.

In the event of effective demand proving chronically insufficient, the operations of the Fund would lead to a piling up of interest-free government obligations. Is there substance in the fear of those who hold that this mounting total would involve a risk of inflation? In principle this should not be so, provided that the size of the deficit is rightly adjusted from time to time. In psychology, however, the matter may be different, and it seems that some guarantee should be furnished. To secure this there are two possibilities. One is that there should be issued some paper of special format, which might be called " savings certificates ", having a guaranteed goods value. If the value of the currency deteriorated, these could be convertible into currency at a premium. The whole of the Budget deficit could be financed by such certificates. There are, however, objections to making a distinction between such savings certificates and ordinary money. If it was not thought desirable to make the distinction, then presumably it would be desirable to guarantee the goods value of the currency itself. I propounded such a scheme in *The Times* last year, with which I will not bother you now.[1] In this scheme the guarantee of the goods value of the currency would be implemented by the issue on demand of goods from buffer stocks. It is to be hoped that we shall have the buffer stocks in any case as a contra-cyclical measure. It would be an elegance if we could link these buffer stocks to the plan for Budget deficits. It might then be possible, as I suggested in the articles, to take all planning decision out of the deficit scheme. The size of the deficit would be automatically regulated by the state of the buffer stocks.

[1] See Appendix.

From a mechanic's point of view there is a beautiful simplicity about this, although to the administrator's mind it may sound complicated, and therefore not very feasible as a practical proposition. Devising automatic self-regulating arrangements of this kind is what I call economic planning. It is something very different, I fear, from planning as commonly discussed.

The only serious published criticism of *The Times* plan was that of Mr. MacDougall who feared that fixing the goods value of the currency would mean depriving the economy of an indispensable safety valve to meet the possibility of excessive money-wage increases. This is no doubt an important point. No danger of this sort appeared to threaten in the period between 1922 and 1939, but matters may not be the same in this respect in the period ahead. If this objection were deemed important, we could confine the guarantee of goods value to the special class of savings certificates. This need not be honoured by tender of goods, but merely by having them convertible into currency at a premium (or discount) varying with the index number of prices. There would thus be a choice open to individuals between holding ordinary currency and holding the certificates with a goods guarantee. Only the former would be legal tender. The two assets would be freely convertible into one another, normally one would hope at par, but, should some inflations of money wages have occurred, at a rate such as to maintain the goods value of the certificates. The certificates would be obtainable, without stamp tax, by all desiring them, in exchange for currency. The Budget deficit, alternatively called " release of money from the Stabilization Fund ", would be equal to the net increase of currency notes during the year plus the net issue of savings certificates.

It might be thought desirable that the banks should be required to take up some or all of the savings certificates. If the public did not at first fancy them, the Budget deficits might lead to a large growth in the volume of bank deposits — since the extra currency notes would be turned into the banks. This would entirely upset the normal ratios of the banks and might lead to some confusion. If they endeavoured to restore their normal proportion of interest-earning assets to cash — they would probably prefer, like the American banks for so long, to carry " excess reserves " — this would greatly enhance their incomes in a way that does not seem justified. One may say this without subscribing to all the fallacies uttered by many of the " 100 per cent money " cranks ! The banks, then, could be required to take up the savings certificates in proportions related to their total assets. But they should not be required to do this, unless their total earning assets were rising, in consequence of the deficit policy, sufficiently to cover the additional expenses of increased turnover. If the gilt-edged rate of interest eventually fell to very low levels, approaching zero, the banks would have to consider covering their expenses by service charges.

I think we must face the possibility that neither deepening nor saving will react sufficiently to a falling interest rate. If at zero interest there were still a re-dundancy of saving, equilibrium could be secured by the continued issue of the savings certificates. The rationale of this would be that certain individuals within the whole community want to exchange present con-sumption for titles to future consumption, to provide for their old age, for their children and all the rest of it. Capitalism, while it was growing rapidly, provided an extraordinarily elegant device by which these wishes could be fulfilled. Would-be transferrers of income to the future could become owners of new physical assets. Since these were productive, interest could be paid. But suppose that the time comes when it is not possible to think of any further assets, or of a sufficiently large number of them, to provide this link between present savings and future income for all those who wish to make the transfer. Must saving come to an end? Surely the right to save, to transfer value that we can consume from the present to a future date or to our descendants, is a freedom fundamental to civilization. The lack of a sufficient number of capital assets to carry this saving forward does not mean that further saving must come to an end, but only that interest must come to an end. In the circumstances suggested, it would be no longer required. Savings would be carried forward by guaranteed savings certificates, having the greatest security that our civilized community can provide for this purpose, through the government; meanwhile, because this large number of people wished to forgo consumption now in exchange for such titles, the community as a whole would be able to consume more than it otherwise could, this extra power of consumption being transferred to it through the reduction of taxation. The scheme is surely quite sensible.

But it has grave social implications on which I would ask you to let your minds dwell for a few minutes at the close of these five lectures. In the concluding section of his *General Theory*,[1] Keynes, in his usual carefree manner, used the memorable and momentous expression " the euthanasia of the rentier ". The context makes it plain that this expression was intended to be taken quite literally. May I quote?

This would not mean that the use of capital instruments would cost almost nothing, but only that the return from them

[1] P. 375.

would have to cover little more than their exhaustion by wastage and obsolescence together with some margin to cover risk and the exercise of skill and judgment. In short, the aggregate return from durable goods in the course of their life would, as in the case of short-lived goods, just cover their labour-costs of production plus an allowance for risk and the costs of skill and supervision.

Now, though this state of affairs would be quite compatible with some measure of individualism [I must put in a gloss here — it strikes me that it would be compatible with a great revival of individualism and plainly call for it], yet it would mean the euthanasia of the rentier, and, consequently the euthanasia of the cumulative oppressive power of the capitalist to exploit the scarcity-value of capital. Interest to-day rewards no genuine sacrifice, any more than does the rent of land. The owner of capital can obtain interest because capital is scarce, just as the owner of land can obtain rent because land is scarce. But whilst there may be intrinsic reasons for the scarcity of land, there are no intrinsic reasons for the scarcity of capital. An intrinsic reason for such scarcity in the sense of a genuine sacrifice which could only be called forth by the offer of a reward in the shape of interest, would not exist, in the long run, except in the event of the individual propensity to consume proving to be of such a character that net saving in conditions of full employment comes to an end before capital has become sufficiently abundant.[1]

I repeat that the approach to this state of society, if ever it comes about, must be gradual and tentative. But still it is something that we should look at with all its implications. It would certainly be a totally new kind of society.

According to my notion, it would be the correct and

[1] In another place (p. 220) Keynes suggests that the rate of interest would be brought to zero within a single generation (presumably thirty years). The destruction caused by the war would require this estimate to be increased somewhat.

final answer to all that is justly advanced by the critics of capitalism. And, because it was the right answer, it would enable us to dispense with the collectivist method of attacking capitalism. What is behind all this collectivism in the hearts of man? It is not really a longing for a totalitarian society. Surely, rather, the collectivist movement has gathered its strength simply because it seemed the only means of displacing the capitalist from " his cumulative oppressive power to exploit the scarcity-value of capital ".

Is not this interest-free society, if we can envisage it not too far beyond the horizon, an alternative to collectivism? Would not the age-long resentment of those who have been downtrodden and suffered be assuaged? Would they not then be prepared to take a different view of free enterprise and its inequality of earnings? Surely it is not the power of the man who does fine work and gets a large measure of profit from it that is resented, so much as the power that he and his descendants have to consolidate themselves on the basis of a large unearned income. We must assume, of course, that there are legal safeguards against his making the profit by exploitation. Could we not thus revive the popular esteem of free enterprise, of profit, yes, of the profit motive itself? Surely it is not the profit itself, earned by service, by assiduity, by imagination, by courage, but the continued interest accruing from the accumulation that makes the profit-taker eventually appear parasitical. Public service, too, should have its high rewards. We have been told that the voting of a large purse to the principal leaders in our recent conflict was contrary to the spirit of the time. I do not believe that this idea has any support in the thoughts of the average man.

As a *quid pro quo*, so to speak, for the " euthanasia ",

it does seem to me most important that large profit should be allowed and encouraged, the corpus of which, if the earner did not want to spend it, could pass on to his children. If there were no unearned income, I suggest that it would be right and fair and widely approved that death duties should be greatly reduced, if not abolished.

If one is making this bold flight of imagination and contemplating a society in which the rentier is no more, then it seems proper that one should dwell for a moment on the virtues of the rentier, very real virtues, although one might not be disposed to pay them so generous a panegyric if death was not in prospect. It is important to recognize how greatly interdependent are the various elements in a civilized society, and, if there is danger of some element disappearing, it is necessary to consider carefully all the functions which it performed, and to take steps to see that they are somehow replaced. That is why I emphasize the importance of large profits and incomes being encouraged and their corpus being transmittable.

Ownership is the foundation of an independent attitude of mind. Owners have not only themselves been in a position to sustain this independent attitude, but also to impose it upon the main body of society. The ideal is that all should have property, and it must be admitted that for generations we have been very far indeed from that ideal. But the influence of ownership in making for independence of mind in the society as a whole must not be underestimated merely because only a few were in that privileged position. It was precisely those few who, because of their position, set the tone, and established a code of right thinking, on which others, less fortunate, based themselves. Political integrity, for generations so high in this country, has been closely related to the independent means of those partaking in political activity. That there should be a class, even if it is only a minority, not dependent for its own livelihood on any political machine, is of the utmost importance for maintaining a high record of honourable dealing in public life and political wisdom.

The existence of this class is also important for the arts and sciences. Of course one may have many highly endowed institutions and many scholarship ladders, but there is no device known to man for the adequate selection of talent, anyhow in the arts. Furthermore we depend for our progress on the emergence of the new idea, like the mutation in natural selection, and standardized methods of selection are likely to miss the type of mind that nourishes it. Indeed the new idea may be genuinely new in the sense that it lies outside the recognized scope of the arts and sciences as catered for by endowment.

There is a further point. The independent class, ultimately the rentier class, whose end we are envisaging, plays a part in developing and defining modes of decent living, what we call civilization. There is an analogy with the concept that we all have of Royalty, which stands before the public as an abstract ideal of perfection. In a minor way the whole class of financially independent people, many, most of whom may in fact supplement their livelihoods by strenuous earning activities, furnish forth a way of living, which both represents what contemporary civilization stands for and provides an aim which everyone may seek to achieve for himself. It provides a target for the ambitious man. To achieve it for oneself, or for that matter for one's children, makes toil and struggle worth while. The capable man may hit the target, many do. But it is also something that, in so far as we are idealists, we wish ultimately everyone to achieve. We wish a general levelling up, not a levelling down. If there is to be a levelling down, if we no longer have an established mode of life that is graceful and charming and delightful, then we take the salt out of socialist hopes. What is the good of a great surge forward for the mass of people, if it is to lead to something not really different in kind from what they had before, to something drab and dreary and without charm or excitement?

I mentioned the question of children. Any degradation of the rentier position touches the population question at a number of places. It is important to keep our eyes open for this. Just because maintenance of the population has been successfully managed for so long, we are apt to take for granted the forces necessary for it, and not to give them explicit attention. We must scrutinize, therefore, such a radical change as that proposed for its implications in this regard.

Taking first the question of excellence, it is probably true to say that fitness for the most important tasks of society cannot be achieved in less than two or three generations. One must always make exception for the man of outstanding genius, who can achieve anything out of nothing. The main positions in all the numerous branches of activity cannot be held by such men alone; there are not enough of them. Life is short, and it is rarely possible to glean in a lifetime all the experience required to make a man of balanced judgment, capable of the higher responsibilities. Experience has to be passed on from father to son. Where the father has made a beginning, has shown himself well fitted for more important tasks than unskilled labour, then it is important that his sons should be regarded as especially qualified candidates for assistance towards further promotion. They have the benefit of their father's lifetime, a benefit which is not enjoyed by, and cannot be made available to, the sons of those who have remained unskilled labourers. It is quite absurd to suppose that we can carry our egalitarian ideas to the point at which all would start from scratch, one with no more advantages than another. Equality of opportunity must be regarded as applying not to each generation in isolation, but as covering a run of generations. The son must start not where his father started, but where his father left off. Of course many sons may prove unworthy of the opportunities thus given them. Such wastage is the price that we have to pay for excellence. If we do not pay, our community will cease to progress and run down to the second-rate or something very much worse.

Secondly, there is also in this matter of excellence the question of heredity. My last argument was based on the idea of the father passing on the fruits of his lifetime experience. There is also the notion that success in life selects good stock. We ought to take advantage of this help given us in the selection of citizens likely in their turn to be able to render valuable service. As an educationist I must stand up for the profound wisdom of examiners, at least at the higher level. But I am bound to recognize how far from perfect examination is as a method of selection; I am sure that much, perhaps most, of our talent would be lost if we relied on that method alone. One must pay tribute of course to the week-end parties so admirably organized by the Civil Service Commissioners. Even they cannot be expected solely to fill the gap. And, anyhow, who will get asked to the parties? There is no doubt much debate and uncertainty about the importance of stock in its influence on the qualities of the individual. I suppose that it cannot be denied that it is supremely important. There is one argument at a popular level that I do not seem to have seen advanced, a very simple argument. Consider the enormous difference between children of the same parents. It is surely impossible that these should be due to difference of environment; these children have almost identical environment. Of course the child a year or two younger may come into the family at a slightly different phase of the parents' success in love or finance. This can hardly account for the enormous differences that we frequently meet with; and they must therefore be due to difference of genetical composition.

There is the counter-argument that qualities making for success in the parents are largely anti-social and therefore undesirable. This is rather a self-defeating maxim. Anyhow in our brave new world we are presumably bent on seeing to it that people with desirable qualities are promoted. But I would also say a word on behalf of the brave old world of three centuries of British development, and thereby of the value of the stock which is found in the upper and middle classes. This is not to deny what I am sure is true, that there is a vast mass of good quality latent in the remainder which can, and should, be raised to higher service by our educational opportunities. Marx of course held that the primary characteristics of these upper and middle classes were those of brigands and exploiters. He has to be confronted with the histories, diaries, letters and novels of these centuries of British history. Taking the whole scene of science, art, industry, efficiency and political management, surely we cannot but believe that the British constitution and mode of civilization have been such that on the whole the leaders have had to have qualities predominantly social and useful. For other countries, some other countries, this argument may have a different moral.

Finally, there is the question of the bare maintenance of numbers. I am convinced that the average size of families will not increase, as it must if we are to avoid extinction, unless those holding the more responsible and noteworthy positions have larger families. It is really rather absurd to ask those who drudge and toil in all other ways also to do the main part of the drudgery in providing the next generation, while those who enjoy more important positions fail to play their proportionate part. One may ask it, but I suggest that it will not happen. And as for these people in responsible positions, I believe that they will not have children merely as so much, I do not say cannon, but merely as so much social fodder. They must have the idea that their children will be valuable and, to some extent, outstanding members of the community. There was the idea, it sounds old-fashioned, but it will have to come back, that the father's own personality was in some sense being carried forward in his children. On that basis he was willing to work and strive in order to give them of his best, but also, and this is important, to have the children. He could feel that his disappointments, his failure to achieve what was in him and express his own personality — and this is the common human lot — would be redeemed by their lives. Of course this attitude has its bad side, excessive possessiveness and a domineering attitude to the children, but this will surely be mitigated by the guiding counsels of our modern psychology. For these reasons it seems necessary that we should have a condition in which parents still can advance their children's interests and promote their welfare and leave them their savings. Thus, if the rentier position is to be liquidated, it is important that as a balancing factor large earnings should be allowed to those who perform good service, and bequest facilitated. With the liquidation of the rentier, in fine, I emphasize the proposal that death duties should be reduced to a minimum, if not abolished altogether.

Thus men would enter life with a corpus of inherited wealth, all, we hope, with some, some with more than others. Altogether the more the better. This would give them freedom of manœuvre, freedom of choice, indeed freedom — for there is truth in that old term used by the critics of capitalism, wage-slaves. The content of freedom is thin and meagre where there is no bank balance. This corpus might normally be used to buy a life annuity, and its owner might set himself the task of saving, sooner or later during his life, from his earnings and the proceeds of the annuity, sufficient to hand on a larger corpus. Or at his choice he might decide to risk it in business enterprise, his own or that of others, to invest it in his own further education or travel, seeking thereby in the end to enlarge it. Most would take one or other of these paths.

But it may be that some, looking deeply into their hearts, would decide otherwise, would decide that they had a task to fulfil in life that would yield no money; for economic activity is not the only good. Perhaps they would devote themselves to public affairs; perhaps they would be artists, students, philanthropists, or perhaps nothing so definite as this, but would go forward obedient to an urge to seek the truth or some special way of life which would satisfy an inner craving, in observing their fellow men at home or abroad — mystics in a modern sense. These are the salt of our society. No doubt there will always be many who, although they have some inspiration of this sort, will none the less have to submit to drudgery. Yet is is important that there should be some who are free to escape from all money earning routine. The church provided for many centuries a status for men of this type, but its dogmas have now closed its doors to most.

Of course their will be a number — not the majority — who dissipate the corpus passed to them in extravagant living of a futile kind. This is the price of freedom and must be tolerated. The cost of a hundred such wastrels is worth incurring for the sake of one man who enriches the life of the community by his example in public life or simply in the art of good life. And if the average humble man who has to earn it all by hard toil cannot be convinced that it is good that there should be some among us who are exempted from such burdens, then, indeed, we may close the book. Democracy will have failed. But he can be convinced.

There has been a debate in academic circles whether income should be distributed equally, according to need, or according to service rendered. I suggest that no one of these criteria will do. One and all, they represent a naïve, almost schoolboy, level of thinking — or, alternatively, since they have been advanced by learned professors, they smell very strongly of the lamp. Precise allocation by need is a recipe of the prison or of the nation at siege. The very stuff of life itself, the interest, the basis of all the charm in life, of romance, of drama depends on variety. Precise allocation by the value of services rendered is little better. The society in which each person drew an income precisely related to his station in the hierarchy would be intolerably vulgar. It would be inconsistent with our canons of refined society, canons which we must not forswear just because reforms are bringing us other good things. In uniform, on the parade ground, everything goes forward according to the precise rank of the officers. In private life the General must meet on equal footing and on equal terms someone who has no General's rank. That makes for and is absolutely necessary to polished behaviour. It is not only that real merit is not to be identified with rewardable merit, although that is an important point. It is also that we need an admixture of persons of no known merit at all. To prove or reinforce my point, I should need qualities other than those of my capacity as an economist, in which I stand before you. I can only refer for evidence and explanation of my meaning to the literature of Britain and France since the renaissance.

You must have it in mind that if in what I have been saying there is a conservative, even a feudal, element, that is to redress the balance in the face of the revolutionary proposal we are considering.

When we come to look closely at the economy free of rentiers, there are no doubt many complications. I will only touch in conclusion upon a few outstanding points.

I take it that new government debt would be free of interest and that the whole debt would gradually be converted on to this basis. At the same time loans could be obtained by entrepreneurs through the banking system free of interest to the limit only of the security that could be offered. The business of life insurance and life annuities would go forward as usual, save that the premiums would have to be somewhat larger in relation to the benefits. Companies would presumably cease paying annual dividends. Anyone actively engaging in a business would expect to receive good profit, whether in the form of a salary as Managing Director or as a rake-off if operating on his own account. Furthermore, those lending money at risk would have the expectation that the corpus of their capital would be enlarged. Companies would declare the value of their assets from time to time and shareholders could sell, whether to reinvest the proceeds in safe interest-free saving certificates or to spend them.

The land is rather an awkward problem. It has been suggested that, owing to the risk element, the price of land would find some natural level at, say, 100 years' purchase. Alternatively at some suitable point on the path towards zero interest, freeholds, and copyholds if any, could be converted into 99-year leaseholds at zero rent, the land being vested, as previously, in the Crown. The conversion would presumably be carried out when we have reached a somewhat lower rate of interest than we have at present. In the interest of continuity, I should like to suggest on behalf of those whose families have been associated with a particular piece of land for generations that on the expiry of the 99 years' lease they should have the first option of renewal for another 99 years, on payment of rent at the then current market evaluation to the Crown. The sentiment now associated with freehold need not be disturbed. It does not seem necessary that land on these long leases should be inalienable.

In the Middle Ages, of course, land was vested in the Crown in this country. It was held by the tenants-in-chief and the rents accrued to them in return for services rendered to the State, mainly of a military character. There were limits to their right to alienate the holdings. The idea occurred to me some time ago that this inalienability was connected with the mediaeval prohibition of usury ; it was certainly necessary as a logical corollary to that prohibition. I argued that the later sophistications of S. Thomas and his followers, which would allow land to have a market value were addressed to reconciling the social revolution proceeding in the later Middle Ages with Christian principles, and represented a departure from earlier more rigorous ideas about interest. On this view the scholastic sophistications would resemble the still more contorted sophistications of the later Jesuits designed to accommodate the rise of modern industry and commerce. But my learned mediaevalist friends assure me that in the most rigorous feudal days land was never really inalienable and unmarketable, and that my pretty picture is nothing more than a private dream of mine. If this is so, it only confirms the view long held by economists, that the mediaeval prohibition of usury never made sense at all and was totally ineffective.

In the conversion of freeholds an exception should be made in favour of endowed institutions. Adam Smith refers to the act of Elizabeth requiring that at least one-third of college endowments should be in corn. This was no doubt in order to safeguard the position of colleges in the new world in which interest was recognized. Earlier, land had been the only vehicle for endowment by respectable persons. Was a William of Wykeham to engage in usury for the benefit of his Foundations? It would be therefore in conformity with mediaeval precedent if land continued to be used as the main vehicle for endowment. And I suggest that this method might be carried a great deal further. Why should not the whole education of the country, not university education only but the whole system, right down to the elementary schools, be placed on a permanent basis of endowment, fortified by the law of the land and severed from State subvention? Only so could we hope to have, taking a long view, a genuinely free education without taint of Fascism or any other form of totalitarianism. Other institutions concerned with the activities of the arts and sciences would qualify for similar endowment.

Have I taken too wide a flight? A very low rate of interest is a fact that we have before us. I suggest that a low rate maintained at a time, such as the present, of unprecedented pressure for new capital is a revolutionary fact. Are there not quite practical intentions that this rate should be further reduced, both here and in the United States? So far we are on firm ground; but how far will this pressure be carried? It can at least do no harm to consider possibilities.

If the Keynesian diagnosis is broadly correct, then this lowering of the rate should bring a new lease of life to private enterprise, and indeed may be the only condition in which it can obtain a new lease of life; for in the last resort public opinion, probably even American public opinion, will not tolerate a system that generates mass unemployment. The other threat to private enterprise lies in socialist opinion, which derives its main strength from resentment at a class of rich conceived as purely parasitical. Talk of the efficiency of State enterprise and the need for co-ordination is largely a cover and recognized by thinking people to be mainly flapdoodle. Is it possible that Socialists may be converted by this idea of an interest-free society and deflected from their tiresome totalitarian proclivities?

What of the United States? It is there that the crucial issue of great unemployment in an economy of free enterprise is likely to appear in a menacing form in the near future. Perhaps these ideas may be considered there first. Is it too much to hope that in their ever-willing desire to experiment the Americans might experiment with them? If they succeeded in operating an interest-free system, then we might also join in, if not too entirely committed meanwhile to the system of collectivism! Thus might we all breathe the air of freedom once more, and other nations too.

APPENDIX

Articles published in *The Times* newspaper on February 7
and February 8, 1946

IF after many years of thinking and brooding upon a problem
an idea comes into one's mind which seems so simple and self-
evident that one cannot understand why it had not been
obvious from the outset, there is a presumption that it is worth
considering. It is such an idea that I propose very briefly to
expound. It consists of a method for maintaining a reasonably
high level of employment.

I present my plan by first referring to two ideas that are
already in the field. One, which was more discussed some
years ago than recently, is that we should endeavour to give
money a stable value in commodities, so that a general fall
in prices, such as occurs in depression, would be impossible,
and thereby the depression itself. At one time it was held that
this might be achieved by the Central Bank using its traditional
methods of Bank rate policy and open market operations, and
zealots in the United States brought the matter to a series of
full discussions before a Congressional Committee in the
'twenties. Expert opinion has inclined to the view that it is
beyond the power of a Central Bank to maintain stability in
the commodity value of a currency by such methods.

One might, however, go further, thereby voyaging in less
familiar waters, and urge that the link with commodities
should be achieved by having the unit of currency made
officially convertible into a standard sample of commodities,
of which the central monetary authority would hold a reserve.
The standard sample would also be convertible into a unit
of currency. This idea, while having attractions to-day as
providing a stockpile of commodities which might have value

for defence purposes, has hitherto been relegated to the category of the merely academic by three objections. First, the cost of storage would be much greater than that of storing gold. (This cost, however, might be accepted, if we could really find a solution of the unemployment problem thereby.) Secondly, there is the fear that the traffic might be all one way, and that the stock-pile would grow and grow without limit. Thirdly, if the commodities included processed articles — and in a British scheme the major part ought to consist of standard processed articles, such as cotton piece goods, steel rails, tin-plate, paint, etc. — there is the danger of obsolescence. The second idea, already in the field, which has had much more vogue just recently, is that the Government should make up a deficiency in the demand for consumption and capital goods by spending additional money on loan account. Public works are prominent in the discussions of this question. I do not doubt that there is a great scope for useful public works in Great Britain. But how big will the gap in work-giving expenditure be that has to be filled? And will the public works be extensive enough to fill it? And are we not in danger of running into absurdity? We do not want to have to think up public works of doubtful utility for the sole purpose of filling the gap. We do not want to dig holes in the ground.

If the gap is considerable, it might be argued, why not fill it the other way? Why not, instead of incurring extra public expenditure on loan account, merely maintain public expenditure at its minimum necessary level and reduce taxation below that level? This would add to total purchasing power. Surely the citizen would rather have the money in his pocket to meet his genuine needs than sponsor public works of doubtful utility.

The objection to this is, of course, the interest charge thrown on to the future taxpayer. So long as a tangible asset, a port installation or trunk road, is created, the charge may be justified. But would it really be right to finance the policeman's wages out of an interest-bearing loan? The advocate

162

of this policy may then say : Why charge interest? Where the increase of purchasing power is genuinely required to make up the balance of employment, why not issue interest-free obligations? And to this again the objection is that it might lead to an outbreak of inflation.

Thus both lines of thought seem to lead to an impasse; but only so long as they are considered separately and in isolation. By combining the two distinct ideas of a currency with a fixed commodity value and of a Budget framed to raise demand to a high employment level, it is possible to remove the fatal objections to each scheme taken in isolation. How might this be done?

A Commodity Reserve would be established. It would consist of goods specified on a list which should be representative of all sections of British production and all localities. Legally and formally one pound sterling would be convertible on demand into a sample consisting of specified quantities of all the goods. In practice, however, the Reserve would usually deal in each article separately. It would set and vary buying and selling prices for each, with a margin of, say, 10 per cent between them, subject to the rule that the selling prices of each must add up to a total equal to the legal price for the sample as a whole, which could only be altered by Act of Parliament. The Reserve would be obliged to buy the commodities at its quoted buying prices without limit of quantity. Thus each branch of industry would be able, when faced by a recession in its business, to reabsorb labour on producing certain standard lines for the Reserve. The Reserve Authority would be linked to the Bank of England in such a way that purchases of goods would entail an expansion of central banking credit and sales a contraction (as is the case with a gold reserve). Its power to vary individual prices would be used by the Authority to keep its holdings of the different commodities in balance. But it would not enable it to influence the growth or shrinkage of the Reserve as a whole. For this the responsibility would fall on the Chancellor of the Exchequer. It would be enacted concurrently that in the event of a persistent tendency for the Commodity Reserve to grow beyond a suitable size, the Chancellor of the Exchequer would be required to supplement the effective purchasing power of the public by remitting taxation, the resulting deficiency being met by the issue of Government obligations interest free. This remission would be continued, and, if necessary, increased, so long as the Commodity Reserve tended to accumulate. If, on the other hand, the opposite tendency set in, he would be obliged not merely to make his Budget balance, but, if necessary, to achieve a surplus for the redemption of debt.

In principle the system would be automatic, Budget deficits being required when the Reserve tended to accumulate and Budget surpluses when it tended to decline. But there would be discretion as to the timing and size of the deficiencies and surpluses. The aim would be to keep the Reserve in equilibrium over a reasonably long period. The main objection to the commodity scheme considered by itself is that the Commodity Reserve might continue to accumulate. But this would clearly be impossible if the Chancellor was bound, when it began to rise too high, to inject into general circulation fresh purchasing power without limit. Sooner or later this additional purchasing power would suffice to keep producers fully employed in supplying the public, thus making any further inflow of goods into the Reserve impossible, and eventually reversing the flow. The fatal objection to relying exclusively on interest-free Exchequer borrowing to secure high employment is that acute inflation might occur before that end was achieved. But if the value of sterling is linked to commodities, inflation is impossible. If there were any tendency for the general level of prices to rise, goods would flow out of the Reserve, and, when this happened, the Chancellor would bring his deficiency spending to an end. Inflation cannot occur if the value of the currency is guaranteed. There would only be deficiency spending when the Commodity

Reserve was abnormally high, that is, when the guarantee could quite certainly be effective.

Thus the two parts of the scheme would give each other mutual support. In the long run the excess of Government expenditure over taxation would be the primary instrument for maintaining high employment in the absence of sufficient demand, the Commodity Reserve being the gauge which regulated the proper amount of this excess. In the short run the Commodity Reserve would be the primary instrument for keeping business active through its obligation to buy a great range of goods without limit of quantity at a given general price level, deficit budgeting being the safety valve which prevented an excessive accumulation of goods in the Reserve.

In the preceding article the bare bones of a plan for maintaining employment at a high level were set out. It is of the essence of the plan that it is self-contained, that it segregates the unemployment problem from wider questions of policy, that it would apply equally well whether the sector of public enterprise is large or small compared with that of private enterprise, and that it would not involve controls or interference with individual producers or merchants in the latter sector. It would only be necessary to begin to operate it when the " transition period " of shortage is over.

A great merit of this plan is that it is entirely consistent with the type of international monetary system proposed at Bretton Woods and now accepted by this country as well as by the United States and others. It would facilitate the working of such a system, since the state of the Commodity Reserve would be a barometer additional to those otherwise available for judging when an adjustment of the country's foreign exchange rates was desirable. If other countries also adopted the plan that would be excellent. But their adoption of it would not be a condition for its adoption here.

Presumably only goods from British production would be accepted by the Reserve Authority save for certain raw materials not produced in this country. But there would be no objection in principle to making foreign goods of similar specification eligible, if the international monetary authority would accept a persistent tendency of foreign goods to accumulate in the Reserve as sufficient evidence that the current foreign exchange rates for sterling were too high and ought to be reduced. The position of gold would not be prejudiced; it would retain its functions as a medium for and reserve against external payments, the Commodity Reserve being held only against internal commitments. The Commodity Reserve might fill a valuable defence rôle. It is not probable that many items on the list would be of strategic importance; and the authority would be obliged to hold suitable quantities of all the goods on the list in order to redeem its obligation to exchange sterling for the standard sample and thus make inflation impossible. But there might be some minimum level below which the Reserve would not be expected to fall, and, within this minimum, there seems no reason why the authority should not hold a disproportionately large quantity of goods of strategic interest. In this way a sizable reserve of materials and food, which it might be thought valuable to have on hand from a defence point of view, could be acquired without cost to the taxpayer.

There is a further advantage in a semi-automatic plan of this kind for securing high employment. It would make it possible to re-establish strict economic canons for judging projects of industrial reconstruction and public expenditure. In spite of adverse factors, it should be possible to achieve a higher standard of living for all in this country after the "transition period". But large prospective increments of national income are already earmarked for various desirable reforms; our position will not be lush; we shall have to eke out our available man-power with careful prudence. It would be most dangerous to slip into the habit of favouring schemes not justifiable on economic grounds merely because they appear likely to "give employment".

APPENDIX

The main practical difficulty in the scheme would be in compiling the list of commodities. In principle all industries and regions should be represented in proportion to their importance in the economy as a whole. But it would not be possible to include goods only made to order, highly specialized articles or branded goods. It would be necessary to select a number of bread-and-butter lines in each trade, in which the various firms could produce to a common specification. This might bias the sample somewhat in favour of " producers' goods ", since so many consumers' goods are branded. This bias would not, however, be harmful, since it is the output of producers' goods that is most subject to fluctuation in accordance with the state of trade, and it is in their case that the compensating effect of the purcheses and releases by the Commodity Reserve would be particularly valuable. Special thought should be given to goods suitable to employ on the spot labour thrown out by a temporary depression in our export markets. Firms producing only types of goods that could not be included would have no ground for grievance, since they would gain from the high employment and high consumption resulting from the scheme. In the long run there would be no special advantage in producing goods on the list, since after the Reserve had been built up its sales would on average be as great as its purchases. In general, Reserve buying prices would tend to be somewhat below the current market prices of the goods. In the case of goods for which an organized market exists it might be necessary to allow the Reserve to buy, in limited quantities only, above its stated buying prices in order to keep up its complement of such goods. In other cases producers, when trade tended to become slack, would be glad to sell at a small percentage below their normal prices in order to maintain turnover.

It is essential that the Reserve should be willing to buy without limit of quantity at its stated buying prices. This standing offer might have an incidental salutary effect, in that it would make it difficult for rings to keep prices much above their competitive level by restrictive agreements. The outsider who could produce a standard line at the official buying price would have as large a market as he required for efficient production. This might well prove a more effective safeguard for the consumer than any anti-trust legislation; with such a safeguard in being public opinion might feel at greater liberty to encourage trade associations and similar bodies in their more beneficent and constructive activities.

If my conviction is correct that with a stationary population the capital outlay required by the community to sustain a rising standard of living will fall considerably short of annual saving, substantial remissions of taxation would continue to be required in order to sustain employment, and the volume of interest-free Government obligations would pile up. The cash and deposits of the banks would grow and these would exert a downward pressure on the rate of interest. This is as it should be. The return on safe investments would fall progressively and enterprise would be stimulated. Whether a new equilibrium would eventually be found at a very low rate of interest who can say? The idea of the large-scale official purchases of commodities is not unfamiliar to-day; still less is that of deficiency budgeting; so that perhaps the ground is not altogether unprepared for the seed of doctrine that I have to offer. But the occasional, *ad hoc* pursuit of such policies will not suffice to guarantee high employment. What is still lacking, but is here suggested, is a body of precise principles to govern and sustain these policies.

Is it too good to be true that a high level of employment could be obtained so simply, by what seems in essence to be a mere mechanical device? It is important to draw a great distinction between the employment question and the standard-of-living question. A higher standard of living can only be achieved in this country if all or most of the individuals in it, fulfilling their respective rôles, produce more, by harder or better work, greater ingenuity and perseverance, greater enterprise and inventiveness, and a more thorough application of scientific method ; and it may be found that the State can help in a variety of ways. There is no short cut to a higher standard of living, and no single recipe. The unemployment question is of a different nature. The involuntary unemployment of able-bodied men or women, when so many needs are unsatisfied, is a mechanical defect in the functioning of our system, and for this kind of evil a mechanical adjustment of the kind proposed is precisely the type of remedy for which we should be seeking.

THE END